Student Workbook

AGS Publishing
Circle Pines, MN 55014-1796
800-328-2560

4201 Woodland Road
Circle Pines, MN 55014-1796
800-328-2560 • www.agsnet.com

AGS Publishing is a trademark and trade name of American Guidance Service, Inc.

Printed in the United States of America

ISBN 0-7854-3861-0

Product Number 94103

A 0 9 8 7 6 5 4 3 2

Table of Contents

Unit 1

Workbook Activity 1 The Earliest Americans
Workbook Activity 2 Peoples of Mesoamerica
Workbook Activity 3 The Early Southwest
Workbook Activity 4 Adena-Hopewell Facts
Workbook Activity 5 Along the Mississippi and to the East
Workbook Activity 6 Ideas of Exploration Begin
Workbook Activity 7 Exploration Continues
Workbook Activity 8 New Colonies Crossword

Unit 2

Workbook Activity 9 Jamestown Puzzle

Workbook Activity 10 The Pilgrims and the Puritans

Workbook Activity 11 Name the Colonies

Workbook Activity 12 The Northern, Middle, and Southern Colonies

Workbook Activity 13 Colonial Trade Vocabulary

Workbook Activity 14 Weighing the Benefits of Colonial Trade

Workbook Activity 15 Western Land Claims

Workbook Activity 16 Details of the French and Indian War

Workbook Activity 17 French and Indian War Crossword

Unit 3

Workbook Activity 18 New British Policies for the Colonies
Workbook Activity 19 Colonial Rebellion
Workbook Activity 20 Understanding the Resistance
Workbook Activity 21 The First Continental Congress
Workbook Activity 22 Preparing to Fight the British
Workbook Activity 23 Congress and General Gage Make Plans
Workbook Activity 24 Revolutionary War Scramble
Workbook Activity 25 Revolutionary War Facts
Workbook Activity 26 Leaders in the War
Workbook Activity 27 Victory Crossword
Workbook Activity 28 A New Nation Faces Problems
Workbook Activity 29 Three Conventions
Workbook Activity 30 Two Plans for a New Government
Workbook Activity 31 Branches of Government Chart
Workbook Activity 32 Federalist or Anti-Federalist?
Workbook Activity 33 Washington and Hamilton
Workbook Activity 34 The Government's Progress
Workbook Activity 35 Adams Administration Crossword
Workbook Activity 36 The Louisiana Purchase
Workbook Activity 37 More Changes Under Jefferson
Workbook Activity 38 Conflicts Continue
Workbook Activity 39 Moving Toward War
Workbook Activity 40 At War with Great Britain
Workbook Activity 41 During or After the War of 1812?

Unit 4

Workbook Activity	42	The United States Expands
Workbook Activity	43	The Era of Good Feelings
Workbook Activity	44	Leaders in the 1820s
Workbook Activity	45	John Q. Adams and Andrew Jackson
Workbook Activity	46	Southern Tension
Workbook Activity	47	Issues During Jackson's Presidency
Workbook Activity	48	Facts About Texan Independence
Workbook Activity	49	The Election of 1836
Workbook Activity	50	How Industry Developed
Workbook Activity	51	Transportation and Communication Crossword
Workbook Activity	52	Immigrant Facts
Workbook Activity	53	Early Education
Workbook Activity	54	Early American Writers
Workbook Activity	55	Early 1840s Timeline
Workbook Activity	56	Events in the Mexican War
Workbook Activity	57	An Election and the Gold Rush

Unit 5

Workbook Activity 58 Debating Slavery
Workbook Activity 59 Slavery Crossword
Workbook Activity 60 The Kansas-Nebraska Act
Workbook Activity 61 Problems in Kansas
Workbook Activity 62 The Issue of Slavery
Workbook Activity 63 Leaders in the Late 1850s
Workbook Activity 64 Political Parties in the 1860 Election
Workbook Activity 65 A New Southern Government
Workbook Activity 66 The Confederates Attack Fort Sumter
Workbook Activity 67 Civil War Crossword
Workbook Activity 68 The Civil War Continues
Workbook Activity 69 Name the General
Workbook Activity 70 Reconstruction Plans and Problems
Workbook Activity 71 Rebuilding the South
Workbook Activity 72 Changes in the South
Workbook Activity 73 The End of Reconstruction

Unit 6

Workbook Activity 74 Railroad Review
Workbook Activity 75 Miners, Cowhands, and Farmers
Workbook Activity 76 Plains Indians Crossword
Workbook Activity 77 Failed Attempts to Help American Indians
Workbook Activity 78 The Industrial Age
Workbook Activity 79 Events in the Development of the Oil Industry
Workbook Activity 80 Inventors and Industry Leaders
Workbook Activity 81 Cities and Factories
Workbook Activity 82 Immigration and Discrimination
Workbook Activity 83 City Living
Workbook Activity 84 City Problems
Workbook Activity 85 Scandals and More Scandals
Workbook Activity 86 Political Reforms Puzzle
Workbook Activity 87 Labor Unions
Workbook Activity 88 The Populist Party

Unit 7

Workbook Activity 89 Problems with Spain
Workbook Activity 90 The Splendid Little War
Workbook Activity 91 The United States and China
Workbook Activity 92 Turn-of-the-Century Crossword
Workbook Activity 93 Roosevelt's Accomplishments in Numbers
Workbook Activity 94 Roosevelt Becomes a Bull Moose
Workbook Activity 95 The War Beings in Europe
Workbook Activity 96 America's Neutral Policy Is Tested
Workbook Activity 97 World War I Crossword
Workbook Activity 98 Wilson's Plan for Permanent Peace
Workbook Activity 99 Presidents Harding and Coolidge
Workbook Activity 100 Social Changes in the Twenties
Workbook Activity 101 The Jazz Age
Workbook Activity 102 Social Problems in the Twenties
Workbook Activity 103 The Rise and Fall of American Confidence

Unit 8

Workbook Activity 104 Causes of the Great Depression

Workbook Activity 105 Hoover or Roosevelt?

Workbook Activity 106 New Deal Crossword

Workbook Activity 107 Escape from the Depression

Workbook Activity 108 The Rise of the Nazi Party in Germany

Workbook Activity 109 Moving Toward a Second World War

Workbook Activity 110 The Beginning of World War II

Workbook Activity 111 War in Asia

Workbook Activity 112 The Home Front

Workbook Activity 113 Germany and Japan Surrender

Unit 9

Workbook Activity 114 A Growing Economy
Workbook Activity 115 War and Peace
Workbook Activity 116 Cold War Crossword
Workbook Activity 117 The Korean War
Workbook Activity 118 Challenges in the 1950s
Workbook Activity 119 The 1960s Begin
Workbook Activity 120 Supporting Freedom Abroad
Workbook Activity 121 Civil Rights Crossword
Workbook Activity 122 The Johnson Administration
Workbook Activity 123 New Movements in America
Workbook Activity 124 The Politics of Protest

Unit 10

Workbook Activity 125 The Vietnam War Moves into Cambodia

Workbook Activity 126 Détente with China and the Soviet Union

Workbook Activity 127 Watergate Crossword

Workbook Activity 128 The Ford Administration

Workbook Activity 129 Problems Around the World

Workbook Activity 130 International Problems Continue

Workbook Activity 131 President Reagan's First Term

Workbook Activity 132 President Reagan's Second Term

Workbook Activity 133 Social Issues and the Bush Administration

Workbook Activity 134 The Fall of Communism

Workbook Activity 135 Gulf War Crossword

Workbook Activity 136 The Clinton Administration

Workbook Activity 137 President Clinton Faces Foreign Issues

Workbook Activity 138 National Issues During the Clinton Years

Workbook Activity 139 New Millennium Crossword

Workbook Activity 140 Terrorism in the United States

Workbook Activity 141 The War on Terror Begins

Workbook Activity 142 What Happened After the War in Iraq?

Workbook Activity 143 The Presidential Candidates of 2004

Workbook Activity 144 The United States Today

Name Date Period

The Earliest Americans

Directions Write the answers to these questions. Use complete sentences.

1. How have we gained knowledge of the first inhabitants of North America?

____

____

____

2. From where did the first inhabitants of North America come? by what route?

____

____

____

3. Where were the oldest traces of American human life found?

____

____

____

4. What hunting tool of the early Americans has been found?

____

____

____

5. As of the year 18,000 B.C., people were no longer able to walk to North America. Why?

____

____

____

Peoples of Mesoamerica

Directions Each sentence below tells about a group of early Mesoamericans. Write the letter of the sentence after the correct name at the bottom of the page.

A The ruins of their temples and pyramids remain as examples of some of the finest building in Mesoamerica.

B These people honored a serpent named Quetzalcoatl.

C They may have settled in Peru as early as 10,000 B.C.

D Their military forces were very strong.

E These people developed an advanced form of writing.

F These people worked as farmers, weavers, or artisans.

G It is believed that nomads overtook them in A.D. 1200.

H They carved in jade and stone.

I These people studied arithmetic and astronomy.

J A hieroglyphic slab written by them is thought to be North America's oldest writing.

K Their main city is now called Mexico City.

L These people started a kingdom in Peru in A.D. 1200.

M Their main city was Tula.

N They were good builders, lawmakers, and warriors.

O These people built many buildings, roads, canals, and bridges.

1. Olmecs ______________________

2. Mayans ______________________

3. Toltecs ______________________

4. Aztecs ______________________

5. Incas ______________________

The Early Southwest

Directions The statements below might have been made by peoples in the early Southwest. Decide which civilization the speaker most likely belonged to. After each statement, write *H* for Hohokam, *M* for Mogollon, *CA* for Chacoan Anasazi, *MVA* for Mesa Verde Anasazi, or *KA* for Kayenta Anasazi.

H	Hohokam
M	Mogollon
CA	Chacoan Anasazi
MVA	Mesa Verde Anasazi
KA	Kayenta Anasazi

1. "We planted at the advice of our sun priests." __________

2. "I played sports in the village court." __________

3. "My brother brought water from the reservoir." __________

4. "My father and I helped build many miles of irrigation canals." __________

5. "Our pit houses were called kivas." __________

6. "Each day we made pottery and weavings." __________

7. "My dress was made from woven cotton." __________

8. "Mother knew the time of year by watching the sun and moon." __________

9. "My civilization began about 200 B.C." __________

10. "We used to live in a pit house, but now we live aboveground." __________

11. "When my uncle died, we covered his head with pottery." __________

12. "Many of my great-grandchildren were Pueblos." __________

13. "Our village has a large court." __________

14. "In the 1300s, my people moved into the Rio Grande area." __________

15. "In 1130, we moved because of a drought." __________

Name ______________________________ Date __________ Period __________

Workbook Activity 4
Chapter 1, Lesson 4

Adena-Hopewell Facts

Directions Write the correct word from the Word Bank to complete each sentence.

Word Bank				
Adena	lizards	mounds	people	rooms
honor	Mississippi	Ohio	rituals	tobacco

1. The Adena dead were first put in small log ______________.

2. The largest Hopewell settlements never had more than

400 ______________.

3. The earliest known Adena people built burial mounds in the

______________ River Valley.

4. The Adena dead were put in burial rooms filled with ______________, pipes, and stone tablets.

5. Many Adena burial ______________ were as large as 300 feet across.

6. The Hopewell people were descendants of the ______________.

7. People in settlements east of the ______________ River traded with the Hopewell.

8. Many other groups of people adopted Hopewell ______________ and customs.

9. Hopewell mounds were built in the shapes of human beings, panthers,

______________, and birds.

10. The Hopewell held burial services to ______________ their dead.

Along the Mississippi and to the East

Directions Circle the letter of the answer that correctly completes each sentence.

1. In the lower Mississippi River Valley, researchers found ______.

A burial grounds **B** corn fields **C** huge pyramids **D** paved roads

2. The first Mississippians ______.

A created painted pottery
B were descendants of the Aztecs
C wove complex patterns
D cultivated plants

3. When people started growing corn, their ______.

A buildings increased in size
B populations increased
C travel increased
D governments grew

4. Cahokia was a ______.

A desert city
B small village
C major trading center
D canyon filled with dwellings

5. The Cherokee, Iroquois, and Natchez are all descendants of ______.

A the Aztecs **B** the Anasazi **C** the Plains Indians **D** the Mississippians

6. Plains Indians traded goods and ideas with the ______.

A Incas **B** Hopewell **C** Mayans **D** Inuit

7. From other people, the Plains Indians adopted ______.

A underground living
B weaving skills
C agriculture and ceremonies
D fishing and government

8. Pacific Northwest civilizations built ______.

A shoreline villages
B cliff villages
C farming villages
D villages around mounds

9. In the Pacific Northwest, most food and trade goods came from ______.

A the forest **B** the ocean **C** crops of vegetables **D** other peoples

10. The sea and caribou provided important goods to the ______.

A Aztec and Incas
B Mississippians
C Eskimo, or Inuit
D Iroquois and Natchez

Name Date Period

Workbook Activity 6
Chapter 2, Lesson 1

Ideas of Exploration Begin

Directions Write the answers to these questions. Use complete sentences.

1. How did jewels, fine silk, perfumes, and spices get from Asia to Europe?

____

____

____

2. Why did people want to find a route to the Far East by sea?

____

____

____

3. How did the compass help sailors?

____

____

____

4. Why was the book about Marco Polo's adventures in China important to explorers?

____

____

____

5. What did Christopher Columbus hope to find when he sailed from Europe?

____

____

____

Name ______ Date ______ Period ______

Workbook Activity **7**
Chapter 2, Lesson 2

Exploration Continues

Directions Match each person or place in Column 1 with a description in Column 2. Write the letter on the line.

Column 1

_____ **1.** Jacques Cartier

_____ **2.** Ferdinand Magellan

_____ **3.** Florida

_____ **4.** Andes Mountains

_____ **5.** Juan Ponce de León

_____ **6.** Philippines

_____ **7.** Hernando Cortés

_____ **8.** Giovanni da Verrazano

_____ **9.** Newfoundland

_____ **10.** Amerigo Vespucci

_____ **11.** Sir Francis Drake

_____ **12.** Montezuma

_____ **13.** Vasco Núñez de Balboa

_____ **14.** John Cabot

_____ **15.** Francisco Pizarro

Column 2

A Magellan was killed here

B determined to conquer the Incas

C America was named for him

D sailed in 1497 and claimed land for England

E sailed in 1524 and reached present-day North Carolina

F looked for the "Fountain of Youth"

G Cabot reached it on his first trip

H conquered the Aztecs

I gold and silver were shipped from mines here

J first European to see the Pacific Ocean from its eastern shore

K Aztec king

L his expedition was the first to sail around the world

M explored the St. Lawrence River

N his expedition was the second to sail around the world

O Spanish word for flower

Name Date Period

New Colonies Crossword

Directions Read each clue. Then choose the correct word from the Word Bank to complete the puzzle.

Word Bank

armada
charter
Croatoan
freedom
Gilbert
Jamestown
loot
Plymouth
Quebec
Raleigh
Roanoke
three
Virginia
west
White

Across

5. shore reached in April of 1607

6. name of company given the second charter by King James

9. clue word carved on a tree on Roanoke Island

10. something people were hoping for in America

13. direction ships sailed from Europe to North America

15. written agreement granting power in the name of a country

Down

1. fleet of warships

2. man given a charter by Queen Elizabeth to start a colony

3. colony named in honor of the king

4. French colony on the St. Lawrence River

7. to take or damage things by force

8. "Lost Colony" settled here

11. man who asked John White to start a colony

12. Virgina Dare's grandfather

14. number of expeditions that Raleigh sent to America

Name Date Period

Workbook Activity 9
Chapter 3, Lesson 1

Jamestown Puzzle

Directions Read each clue. Choose a word from the Word Bank to complete the puzzle. Then write the answer from the box.

1. | __ | __ __ __ __ __ __ __ __ __ __
2. __ | __ | __ __ __ __ __ __ __ __
3. __ __ __ __ | __ | __ __ __
4. __ __ __ __ | __ |
5. | __ | __ __ __ __ __ __
6. __ __ __ __ | __ | __ __
7. __ __ __ __ __ __ __ __ | __ | __ __ __ __ __ __
8. __ __ | __ | __ __
9. __ | __ | __ __ __ __ __ __
10. __ __ __ __ __ __ | __ |

1. John Rolfe married a young American Indian woman named ______.
2. The Jamestown colonists built a ______ for protection.
3. The ______ tribe helped the colonists.
4. In 1619, the Virginia Company sent 90 single ______ to marry the settlers.
5. John Rolfe planted ______.
6. ______ killed many of Jamestown's early settlers.
7. Settlers chose ______ to serve in the House of Burgesses.
8. Captain John ______ said that every person had to work to eat.
9. Lord Delaware became ______ of the colony.
10. In 1619, the first ______ slaves came to America.

Word Bank

African
blockhouse
disease
governor
Pocahontas
Powhatan
representatives
Smith
tobacco
women

What word do the letters in the box spell? ______________________

Name Date Period

Workbook Activity 10
Chapter 3, Lesson 2

The Pilgrims and the Puritans

Directions Write the answers to these questions. Use complete sentences.

1. What is a stock company?

2. Who were the Pilgrims?

3. Where did the Pilgrims first escape to?

4. Where was the Mayflower supposed to land? Where did it land?

5. What was the Mayflower Compact?

6. Why couldn't the Pilgrims attract more settlers?

7. Why did the Puritans leave England in 1629?

8. How did the Puritans prepare for their journey to America?

9. How large was the first group of Puritans that came to Boston?

10. Compare the Pilgrims and Puritans. How were they alike? How were they different?

Name the Colonies

Directions Fill in the chart. Write the 13 original colonies in the order in which they were started. Then write the date that each colony was started. The first two have been done for you.

Colony	Date Started
1. Virginia (Jamestown)	1607
2. Massachusetts (Plymouth)	1620
3.	
4.	
5.	
6.	
7.	
8.	
9.	
10.	
11.	
12.	
13.	

Name Date Period

The Northern, Middle, and Southern Colonies

Directions Complete the chart. Write the name of each colony from the Word Bank in the correct column below.

Word Bank

Connecticut	Rhode Island	Maryland
New Hampshire	Georgia	North Carolina
Pennsylvania	New York	Virginia
Delaware	South Carolina	Massachusetts
New Jersey		

Northern Colonies	Middle Colonies	Southern Colonies
1. ________	**5.** ________	**9.** ________
2. ________	**6.** ________	**10.** ________
3. ________	**7.** ________	**11.** ________
4. ________	**8.** ________	**12.** ________
		13. ________

Directions Write one fact that describes each of the following groups of colonies.

14. Northern colonies

____

____

15. Middle colonies

____

____

16. Southern colonies

____

____

Colonial Trade Vocabulary

Directions Read each numbered statement. Choose the best meaning for each underlined word from the Answer Bank. Write the meaning on the lines.

Answer Bank

- having to do with the arts
- to govern, or direct, according to a rule
- the need to complete duties or tasks
- ability to take care of oneself
- people elected to serve in government

1. Colonists wanted to take responsibility for their own success.

____

____

2. Great Britain did not want the colonies to feel an independence.

____

____

3. The cultural life of people in the colonies developed quickly.

____

____

4. Delegates were in charge of making laws.

____

____

5. The colonists wanted to regulate trade for themselves.

____

____

Name Date Period

Workbook Activity 14
Chapter 4, Lesson 2

Weighing the Benefits of Colonial Trade

Directions Each trading fact in the Answer Bank benefited either the colonies or Great Britain. Write each fact under the correct heading below.

Answer Bank

- Africa wanted goods made in New England.
- Great Britain passed the Navigation Acts between 1651 and 1673.
- Africans were captured and brought to America as slaves.
- The British took steps to enforce their laws.
- A tax was added to molasses from the West Indies.
- The colonists bought goods from Great Britain.
- Triangular trade formed between New England, Africa, and the West Indies.
- Some British officials in the colonies were paid to look the other way.
- The number of colonists from Sweden, the Netherlands, Germany, and Ireland was increasing.
- The Woolens Act was passed in 1699.

Benefited the Colonies	Benefited Great Britain

Name Date Period

Workbook Activity
Chapter 4, Lesson 3
15

Western Land Claims

Directions Write the answers to these questions. Use complete sentences.

1. What countries had claims in the Ohio Valley?

______

______

______

2. Why was George Washington first sent to visit the Ohio Valley?

______

______

______

3. What was the purpose of the Albany Congress?

______

______

______

4. What advantages did the British in the Ohio Valley have over the French?

______

______

______

5. What advantages did the French in the Ohio Valley have?

______

______

______

Name Date Period

Workbook Activity 16
Chapter 4, Lesson 4

Details of the French and Indian War

Directions Match each item in Column 1 with a detail in Column 2. Write the letter on the line.

Column 1

______ **1.** William Henry

______ **2.** King George II

______ **3.** cooperation

______ **4.** survivor

______ **5.** Ohio Valley

______ **6.** George Washington

______ **7.** William Pitt

______ **8.** Crown Point

______ **9.** Louisbourg

______ **10.** General Braddock

______ **11.** American colonists

______ **12.** Duquesne

______ **13.** American Indians

______ **14.** confidence

______ **15.** France

Column 2

A prime minister of Great Britain

B what colonists gained after Pitt's changes to the British army

C fort in New York

D French naval base in Nova Scotia

E fought alonside the French at Fort Duquesne

F fought alongside the British

G suggested ways General Braddock should prepare for battle

H what William Pitt gained by encouraging the colonists

I someone who has lived through danger

J important valley that the British and French wanted to control

K surprise attack happened near this fort

L British monarch

M had little respect for American Indians as warriors

N British lost many men in a failed battle at this fort

O joined the American Indians in a war against the British

Name Date Period

Workbook Activity 17
Chapter 4, Lesson 5

French and Indian War Crossword

Directions Read each clue. Then choose the correct word from the Word Bank to complete the puzzle.

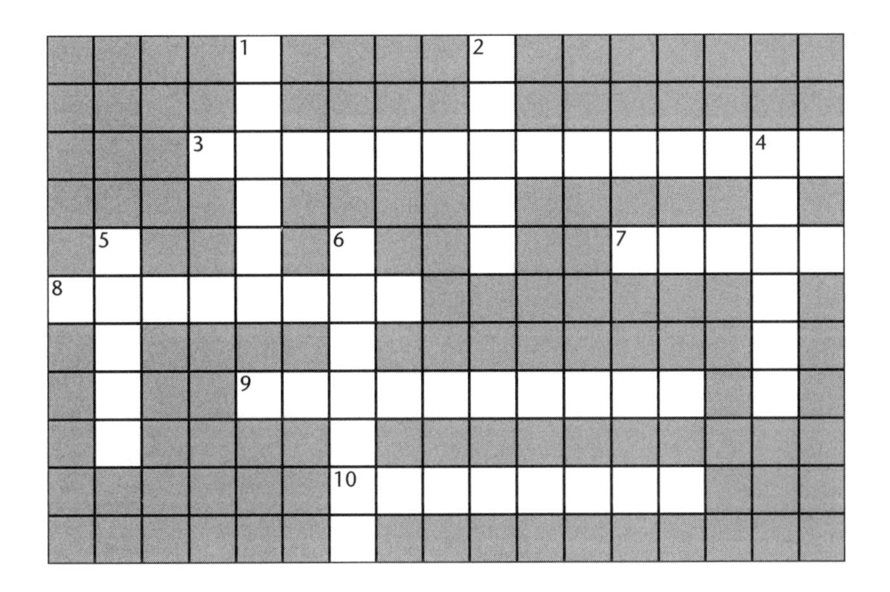

Word Bank

Duquesne
Florida
Montcalm
Paris
Quebec
reinforcements
stronghold
taxes
treaty
Wolfe

Across

3. Additional soldiers used to back up an army are called ______.

7. ______ would be raised to pay for the war.

8. ______ was the French leader at the Battle of Quebec.

9. A ______ is a place well protected from attack.

10. The capture of Fort ______ was a turning point in the war.

Down

1. ______ was a French stronghold protected by high cliffs.

2. The Treaty of ______ ended the war.

4. A ______ is an agreement to end fighting.

5. British leader James ______ died at Quebec.

6. Spain gave ______ to Great Britain in exchange for Cuba.

New British Policies for the Colonies

Directions Write the answers to these questions. Use complete sentences.

1. How did Great Britain try to control the American colonies after the French and Indian War?

____

____

____

2. Who was Chief Pontiac?

____

____

____

3. Why did Americans think that the Proclamation of 1763 was unfair?

____

____

____

4. How did Great Britain set out to raise money after the war?

____

____

____

5. What was the purpose of the Stamp Act?

____

____

____

Colonial Rebellion

Directions Write the correct word from the Word Bank to complete each sentence.

Word Bank	
boycotted	repealed
Crispus Attucks	responsible
finance	Samuel Adams
jobs	taxation
Liberty	troops

1. Great Britain's minister of ____________________ was Charles Townshend.

2. Townshend was ____________________ for a new set of tax laws.

3. Trade slowed down because colonists ____________________ British goods.

4. Colonists lost ____________________ in ports where trade was important.

5. Boston became the center of action against British policies

of ____________________.

6. The Sons of ____________________ took charge of Boston.

7. In order to protect its tax collectors, Britain sent regiments

of ____________________.

8. The soldiers who fired into the crowd killed ____________________ and other colonists.

9. After the Boston Massacre, all of the Townshend taxes were

____________________ except for the tax on tea.

10. ____________________ encouraged the colonists to band together in opposing the British.

Name Date Period

Workbook Activity **20**

Chapter 5, Lesson 3

Understanding the Resistance

Directions Circle the letter of the answer that correctly completes each sentence.

1. The _______ allowed Great Britain to close the port of Boston to all trade.

A duty on tea

B East India Trading Company

C Quebec Act

D Intolerable Acts

2. The colonists refused to pay the tea tax because they _______.

A feared American merchants would go out of business

B wanted a tax on sugar instead of tea

C disliked Frederick North, British prime minister

D knew that the tea was rotten

3. The people who threw the tea overboard in Boston's harbor were _______.

A upset with American merchants

B angry with the ship captain

C dressed as Mohawk Indians

D British merchants

4. In Charleston, South Carolina, the tea that was brought from Great Britain was _______.

A burned **B** left to rot **C** sent back **D** thrown in the water

5. The Quebec Act was designed to keep colonists out of _______.

A Massachusetts **B** the city of Quebec **C** the Ohio Valley **D** South Carolina

6. The Intolerable Acts said that British soldiers accused of breaking the law would be _______.

A moved to Maryland **B** tried in Great Britain **C** put in American jails **D** tried by the colonists

7. Lord North wanted to stop the East India Trading Company from _______.

A paying a tax **B** paying a fine **C** losing tea **D** selling tea

8. American merchants reacted to the tea tax by _______.

A selling coffee instead **B** increasing tea prices **C** ordering more tea **D** canceling tea orders

9. After the Boston Tea Party, some American merchants _______.

A offered to pay for the tea that was destroyed

B ordered more tea from Great Britain

C wanted Great Britain to increase the duty on tea

D were afraid they would not be able to buy tea

10. The British responded to the Boston Tea Party by _______.

A reducing the duty on tea

B offering better tea to American merchants

C passing the Intolerable Acts

D hiring new ship captains

The First Continental Congress

Directions Match the words in Column 1 with the details in Column 2. Write the letter on the line.

Column 1

_____ **1.** Concord

_____ **2.** Samuel Adams

_____ **3.** minutemen

_____ **4.** William Dawes

_____ **5.** John Hancock

_____ **6.** Philadelphia

_____ **7.** patriots

_____ **8.** Lexington

_____ **9.** General Gage

_____ **10.** Second Continental Congress

_____ **11.** Great Britain's king

_____ **12.** Major Pitcairn

_____ **13.** Samuel Prescott

_____ **14.** John Jay

_____ **15.** Massachusetts

Column 2

A military governor of Massachusetts

B where the First Continental Congress was held

C he and Parliament were furious about the Declaration of Rights

D warned the colonists in Concord that the British were coming

E attended the First Continental Congress

F decided to call a meeting of colonial representatives

G would be held if the king rejected the Declaration of Rights

H he, Patrick Henry, and Samuel Adams were sure the colonists would have to fight for freedom

I where colonists met the British

J Paul Revere rode through it on horseback

K leader of the British regiment that marched to Lexington

L he and Paul Revere warned the colonists

M where military supplies were stored

N people who love their own country

O colonial soldiers who could gather quickly

Name Date Period

Preparing to Fight the British

Directions Write the answers to these questions. Use complete sentences.

1. In what ways did the fighting at Lexington and Concord affect the colonists?

____

____

____

2. What did the colonists do to prevent the British from disarming them?

____

____

____

3. What did Ethan Allen and his Green Mountain Boys do to help the colonists?

____

____

____

4. Why was May 10, 1775, an important date in American history?

____

____

____

5. What did many colonists do in an effort to keep the peace?

____

____

____

Congress and General Gage Make Plans

Directions Write the answers to these questions. Use complete sentences.

1. What did the delegates agree that Congress could and could not do?

____

____

____

2. How did Congress choose the chief commander of the army? Whom did they choose?

____

____

____

3. What else did Congress do as a central governing body?

____

____

____

4. How did General Gage respond to the American soldiers setting up camp near Boston?

____

____

____

5. How did General Gage plan to protect Dorchester Heights?

____

____

____

Name Date Period

Workbook Activity
Chapter 6, Lesson 3
24

Revolutionary War Scramble

Directions Write the correct word from the Word Bank to complete each sentence. Then unscramble the circled letters to answer question 10.

Word Bank		
British	invade	orator
clause	loyalists	Quebec
document	Montreal	statesman

1. The ___ (___) ___ ___ ___ ___ ___ formed an army in Canada.

2. Congress did not want the British to (___) ___ ___ ___ ___ ___ New York from the north.

3. General Montgomery captured (___) ___ ___ ___ ___ ___ ___ ___.

4. ___ ___ (___) ___ ___ ___ was not an easy Canadian city to capture.

5. The American soldiers defeated ___ ___ ___ (___) ___ ___ ___ ___ ___ at Moore's Creek, North Carolina.

6. A(n) (___) ___ ___ ___ ___ ___ ___ ___ ___ is someone who knows and practices government ideas.

7. Patrick Henry was a(n) ___ ___ (___) ___ ___ ___ and a statesmen.

8. The original Declaration of Independence had a slave (___) ___ ___ ___ ___ ___.

9. Some of the delegates refused to sign the ___ ___ ___ ___ ___ ___ (___) ___ unless it was changed.

10. What did the colonists become when they separated from Great Britain?

____

Name Date Period

Revolutionary War Facts

Directions Write the correct word from the Word Bank to complete each sentence.

Word Bank	
Americans	pardon
Boston	revolution
British	siege
Hessians	Trenton
Nathan Hale	William Howe

1. George Washington didn't want the ______________________ to take over New York harbor.

2. A(n) ______________________ is the act of overthrowing and replacing a government.

3. General ______________________ and his brother reached Staten Island.

4. King George III said he would ______________________ anyone who surrendered.

5. Nathan Hale proved himself at New York as he had earlier at ______________________.

6. ______________________ said, "I only regret that I have but one life to lose for my country."

7. A(n) ______________________ is when an army prevents people from leaving a city.

8. On December 25, 1776, Washington attacked ______________________, New Jersey.

9. The British hired a group of soldiers called ______________________.

10. The ______________________ defeated three enemy regiments at Princeton.

Name Date Period

Leaders in the War

Directions The statements below might have been made by people during the turning point of the Revolutionary War. Decide which person could have made each statement. After each statement, write *W* for George Washington, *H* for General Howe, *F* for Benjamin Franklin, *C* for George Rogers Clark, or *G* for Horatio Gates.

W	George Washington
H	General Howe
F	Benjamin Franklin
C	George Rogers Clark
G	Horatio Gates

1. "Governor Henry has called me into service." __________

2. "We must stop Howe's men from taking Philadelphia." __________

3. "After our victory at Saratoga, the French agreed to answer my plea." __________

4. "I was called to Great Britain in 1778." __________

5. "I know the Ohio Valley well." __________

6. "We contained the British at New York." __________

7. "General Burgoyne, I accept your surrender." __________

8. "They didn't make it to Philadelphia—we stopped them at Germantown." __________

9. "I regret that I did not send reinforcements from the south." __________

10. "We set up our quarters at Valley Forge." __________

11. "We have captured Vincennes." __________

12. "I came to Paris to ask for your help." __________

13. "We moved on to capture Cahokia." __________

14. "Yes, we won the battle at Saratoga." __________

15. "Often my troops had to remain unpaid." __________

Name Date Period

Victory Crossword

Directions Read each clue. Then choose the correct word from the Word Bank to complete the puzzle.

Word Bank

André
Arnold
boundaries
Cornwallis
Florida
Greene
lure
naval
plans
redeem
Saratoga
Serapis
traitor
Treaty
victory

Across

3. A(n) _______ turns against his or her country.

5. _______ was supposed to deliver takeover plans.

9. John Paul Jones's _______ is still an example.

10. Benedict Arnold fought bravely at _______ and Quebec.

12. Lord Cornwallis wanted to _______ himself after losing inland positions.

14. John Paul Jones captured the warship _______.

15. Nathaniel Greene was able to _______ the British into North Carolina.

Down

1. The _______ of Paris ended the Revolutionary War.

2. Great Britain was forced to return _______ to Spain.

4. _______ invaded Virginia, but was pushed back.

6. _______ plotted to turn over West Point.

7. In 1783, America's new _______ were established.

8. _______ were hidden in John Andre's boots.

11. _______ recaptured inland positions from the British.

13. John Paul Jones became a great _______ hero.

A New Nation Faces Problems

Directions Write the answers to these questions. Use complete sentences.

1. Why did American settlers have trouble getting help fighting the Indians or Spanish?

2. Why did Americans need new trading partners?

3. Spain refused to allow Americans to ship goods from New Orleans. Why didn't the United States force Spain to change its policy?

4. In what ways did states treat one another as separate countries? How did this hurt the new American nation?

5. In what ways was Congress weak under the Articles of Confederation?

Three Conventions

Directions Read each statement. Decide which convention it describes. After each statement, write *A* for the Annapolis Convention, *M* for the Mount Vernon Convention, or *C* for the Constitutional Convention.

M	Mount Vernon Convention
A	Annapolis Convention
C	Constitutional Convention

1. Its purpose was to create a stronger government. __________

2. It met at George Washington's home. __________

3. It was held in Philadelphia. __________

4. It settled a dispute over commercial rights on the Potomac River. __________

5. It was proposed by James Madison. __________

6. Its sessions were held in secrecy. __________

7. It was held to settle a dispute between Maryland and Virginia. __________

8. Only five states sent delegates. __________

9. Twelve states sent delegates. __________

10. It was held in Maryland. __________

Name Date Period

Two Plans for a New Government

Directions Circle the letter of the answer that correctly completes each sentence.

1. The Constitutional Convention first met to ________.

A create a new system of government
B copy the government of Great Britain
C adjust the Articles of Confederation
D rewrite the Declaration of Independence

2. ________ presented the Virginia Plan.

A Thomas Jefferson **B** Edmund Randolph **C** William Paterson **D** George Washington

3. In the Virginia Plan, ________.

A each state had equal votes
B smaller states had more representatives
C larger states had more representatives
D only the large states had representatives

4. In the Virginia Plan, Congress was supposed to ________ the laws.

A make **B** enforce **C** judge **D** change all

5. In the Virginia Plan, a court system was to ________.

A guarantee justice
B enforce the laws
C make the laws
D have state representatives

6. ________ presented the New Jersey Plan.

A Thomas Jefferson **B** Edmund Randolph **C** William Paterson **D** George Washington

7. The New Jersey Plan called for ________.

A a stronger central government
B state representatives based on population
C less state control
D greater state control

8. The small-state plan called for something ________ the government that already existed.

A much like **B** very different from **C** much bigger than **D** much smaller than

9. Benjamin Franklin and ________ provided wisdom and encouraged the delegates to compromise.

A Thomas Jefferson **B** Edmund Randolph **C** William Paterson **D** George Washington

10. A deadlock is when two groups ________.

A agree about everything
B cannot agree on something
C compromise their opinions
D refuse to vote

Branches of Government Chart

Directions Each detail in the Answer Bank describes one of the branches of government. Write each detail under the correct heading below.

Answer Bank

- has a chief justice
- consists of elected representatives
- enforces laws
- receives help from advisers
- includes the House of Representatives
- interprets laws
- makes laws
- includes the president
- includes the Senate
- includes the Supreme Court

Legislative Branch	Judicial Branch	Executive Branch

Name Date Period

Federalist or Anti-Federalist?

Directions Each detail in the Answer Bank describes either the Federalists or the Anti-Federalists. Write each detail under the correct heading below.

Answer Bank

- were led by Alexander Hamilton in New York
- feared that state governments would be destroyed
- felt that the Constitution gave the central government too much power
- were led by James Madison and John Marshall in Virginia
- supported an increase in the central government's power
- thought the Constitution did not favor farmers
- wrote and circulated essays to explain the Constitution
- were led by Patrick Henry and George Mason in Virginia
- supported the Constitution
- thought the Constitution did not provide for protection of personal freedoms

Federalists	Anti-Federalists

Washington and Hamilton

Directions Write the answers to these questions. Use complete sentences.

1. Who did George Washington choose to be his advisers?

____

____

____

2. At the end of the Revolutionary War, what was the problem with the United States treasury?

____

____

____

3. Why did many in Congress dislike Alexander Hamilton's financial plan?

____

____

____

4. Why do you think the capital was moved from New York to Washington, D.C.?

____

____

____

5. What were some of the results of Hamilton's financial plan?

____

____

____

The Government's Progress

Directions Write the correct word from the Word Bank to complete each sentence.

Word Bank	
American Indians	George Washington
debt	neutral
Democratic-Republican Party	Spain
Federalist Party	term
Florida	treaty

1. Those who favored Alexander Hamilton's ideas made up the

______________________.

2. The ______________________ supported stronger state government.

3. ______________________ believed that opposing political parties could cause more disagreement.

4. The United States could not go to war again because of its

______________________.

5. When France and Great Britain went to war, President Washington decided the United States should remain ______________________.

6. Great Britain had been selling firearms to ______________________.

7. John Jay went to London to discuss a ______________________.

8. In 1795, ______________________ permitted Americans to use the Mississippi River and New Orleans for trade.

9. Spain gave the United States a section of ______________________.

10. Washington agreed to serve a second ______________________.

Adams Administration Crossword

Directions Read each clue. Then choose the correct word from the Word Bank to complete the puzzle.

Word Bank

- alien
- Burr
- central
- deport
- Federalist
- France
- Hamilton
- press
- Sedition
- tie

Across

2. The Constitution provides for freedom of speech and freedom of the _______.

3. _______ got the same number of votes as Jefferson.

5. The election of 1800 resulted in a(n) _______.

7. _______ influenced Congress about the final presidential choice.

9. X, Y, and Z were secret agents of _______.

10. A(n) _______ lives in one country but is a citizen of another.

Down

1. The Alien Act gave the government the right to _______ an alien.

4. The _______ Act made it a crime to speak out against the government.

6. John Adams supported a strong _______ government.

8. John Adams belonged to the _______ Party.

The Louisiana Purchase

Directions Match the words in Column 1 with the details in Column 2. Write the letter on the line.

Column 1

_____ **1.** Napoleon Bonaparte

_____ **2.** France

_____ **3.** New Orleans

_____ **4.** Robert Livingston

_____ **5.** West Point

_____ **6.** James Monroe

_____ **7.** Virginia

_____ **8.** Thomas Jefferson

_____ **9.** Minnesota

_____ **10.** Mississippi River

_____ **11.** District of Columbia

_____ **12.** Louisiana Purchase

_____ **13.** Spain

_____ **14.** Federalists

_____ **15.** Congress

Column 2

A present-day state that was part of the Louisiana Territory

B where Thomas Jefferson was inaugurated

C was forced to return Louisiana

D opposed the Louisiana Purchase

E country from which America bought the Louisiana Territory

F French leader

G important port for international trade

H American ambassador

I sent to Paris by Jefferson

J believed the Constitution controlled government

K approved the Louisiana Purchase in 1803

L waterway gained by the Louisiana Purchase

M Jefferson's home state

N doubled the size of America

O site of the United States Military Academy

Name Date Period

More Changes Under Jefferson

Directions Circle the letter of the answer that correctly completes each sentence.

1. President Jefferson sent Meriwether Lewis and William Clark to explore parts of the ______.

A Mississippi River **B** Southwest **C** Louisiana Territory **D** state of Florida

2. ______ was a guide for Lewis and Clark.

A Zebulon Pike **B** Thomas Jefferson **C** John Marshall **D** Sacajawea

3. Zebulon Pike was looking for the source of the ______.

A Mississippi River **B** Pacific Ocean **C** Gulf of Mexico **D** Columbia River

4. Great Britain and ______ were at war again.

A Canada **B** Spain **C** the United States **D** France

5. A ______ stops goods and people from entering a country.

A boycott **B** blockade **C** treaty **D** tariff

6. Congress passed the Embargo Act to ______.

A stop American trade with foreign countries

B encourage American trade with foreign countries

C help American shippers

D help manufacturers of American-made goods

7. The Embargo Act was a ______.

A disagreement **B** success **C** failure **D** blockade

8. John Marshall was chief justice of ______.

A Virginia's court system

B the president's Cabinet

C Washington, D.C.

D the Supreme Court

9. The decision in *Marbury v. Madison* said that the judicial department must ______ the law.

A enforce **B** explain **C** make **D** change

10. John Marshall helped make sure the ______ could meet the changing needs of the nation.

A Embargo Act **B** Louisiana Territory **C** Constitution **D** presidency

Name Date Period

Conflicts Continue

Directions Write the answers to these questions. Use complete sentences.

1. What new policy did President Madison propose?

____

____

____

2. How would Great Britain be affected if Americans closed their ports to the British?

____

____

____

3. What did the "War Hawks" of the 12th Congress want?

____

____

____

4. What ongoing problem did American ships face?

____

____

____

5. What was the difference between America's relationship with Great Britain and America's relationship with France?

____

____

____

Name Date Period

Moving Toward War

Directions Write the correct word from the Word Bank to complete each sentence.

Word Bank	
action	industries
defeated	interfered
doubled	organize
established	standstill
frontier	support

1. When James Madison became president, 20 years had passed since the Constitution ______________ the new government.

2. By 1810, the area of the United States had ______________ in size.

3. While the southern states were producing cash crops, the New England states were developing ______________.

4. The ______________ was being pushed farther west.

5. The War Hawks believed it was time for Americans to take

______________.

6. Henry Clay and John C. Calhoun thought Canada could easily be

______________.

7. The British had seized American ships and ______________ with trade.

8. Tecumseh tried to ______________ a confederacy against settlers.

9. America had no money to ______________ a well-trained army.

10. Foreign trade had almost come to a complete ______________.

At War with Great Britain

Directions Circle the letter of the answer that correctly completes each sentence.

1. _______ declared war against Great Britain.

A Captain Perry **B** DeWitt Clinton **C** President Madison **D** Congress

2. The War Hawks supported Madison for president in 1812 because he wanted to _______.

A have peace
B trade with Great Britain
C go to war with Great Britain
D trade with France

3. American attempts to invade Canada _______.

A were aided by Tecumseh
B resulted in defeats
C were led by Andrew Jackson
D resulted in victories

4. Great Britain created a _______ to stop all shipping to and from the United States.

A blockade **B** treaty **C** contest **D** warship

5. The victory on Lake Erie was important because _______.

A it allowed America to invade Canada
B it opened American trade with France
C it stopped the British from invading the Ohio Valley
D it meant that Great Britain would lose the war

6. At the Battle of the Thames in Canada, Americans _______.

A cooperated with Tecumseh
B defeated the British
C were defeated by the British
D took Tecumseh prisoner

7. _______ defeated the Creeks at Horseshoe Bend in early 1814.

A DeWitt Clinton **B** General Harrison **C** Captain Perry **D** Andrew Jackson

8. The British returned to Canada after the Battle of Lake Champlain because they _______.

A gave up hope of capturing New York
B easily defeated the tiny American fleet
C lost the help of the Shawnees
D needed new supplies and men

9. _______ burned the capitol building and the White House.

A The Shawnees **B** The Canadians **C** The British **D** The War Hawks

10. The British tried to capture Baltimore, Maryland, by _______.

A shelling Fort McHenry
B attacking the capitol building
C marching through Washington, D.C.
D controlling Lake Erie

During or After the War of 1812?

Directions Each fact in the Answer Bank describes either the time period during the war or the time period after the Treaty of Ghent. Write each fact under the correct heading below.

Answer Bank

- Support for the war was mixed.
- Westward expansion was safer.
- Spending was increased.
- A battle at New Orleans was fought.
- Territory and possessions taken during the war were to be returned.
- The need to be self-sufficient grew.
- Trade was nearly ruined.
- American Indians signed a treaty to give up land.
- Andrew Jackson's popularity spread throughout the land.
- America had a new sense of nationalism.

During the War of 1812	After the Treaty of Ghent

The United States Expands

Directions Read each clue. Then choose the correct word from the Word Bank to complete the puzzle.

Word Bank

- Alabama
- Canal
- cotton
- Federalists
- frontier
- Indiana
- Madison
- Monroe
- season
- slaves

Across

1. President James _______ was elected in 1816.
2. The _______ were finished as a political party.
7. New Englanders could travel west on the Erie _______.
8. Eli Whitney invented the _______ gin.
9. The western state of _______ joined the Union in 1816.

Down

1. President James _______ was very popular at the end of his second term.
3. _______ became a new state in the South in 1819.
4. The South had a long growing _______.
5. The number of _______ increased in the South.
6. A new spirit of nationalism grew in the western _______ states.

Name Date Period

Workbook Activity 43
Chapter 10, Lesson 2

The Era of Good Feelings

Directions Read each clue. Choose a word from the Word Bank to complete the puzzle. Then write the answer from the box.

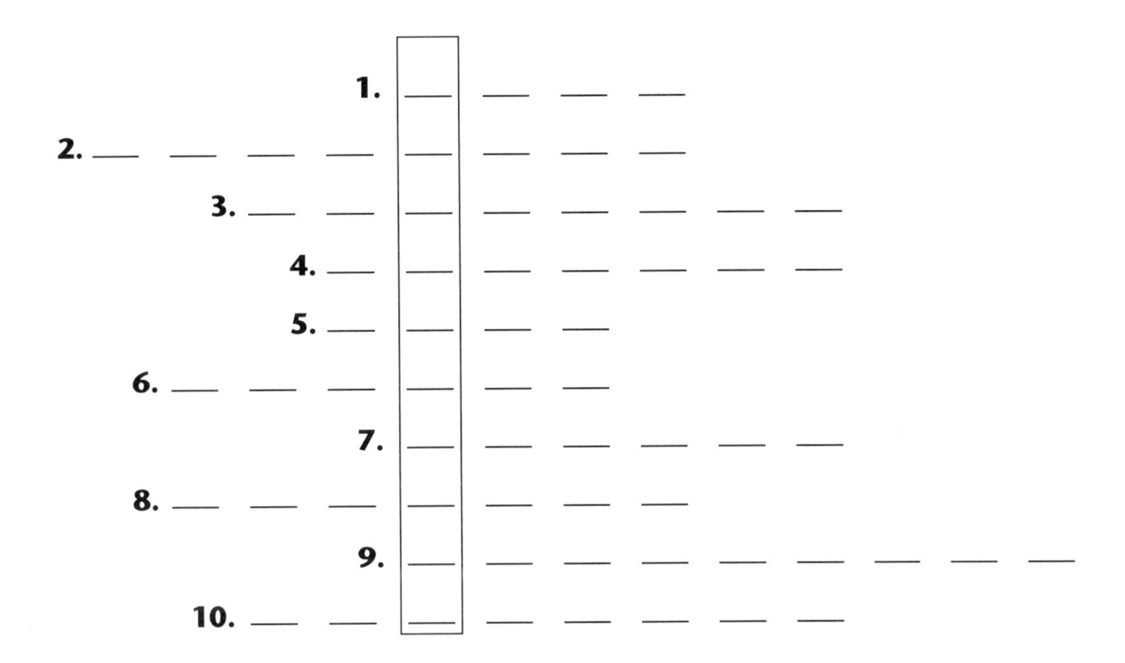

1. Henry _______ was known as the "Great Compromiser."

2. _______ entered the Union as a slave state.

3. General Andrew Jackson invaded _______ country.

4. The _______ gave all of Florida to the United States.

5. Maine entered the union as a _______ state.

6. A slave _______ was planned in South Carolina.

7. President _______'s two terms were called the Era of Good Feelings.

8. The President's _______ had people from different parts of the country.

9. Many _______ differences were increasing in the country.

10. Denmark Vesey and 35 other people were _______.

What word do the letters in the box spell? ___________________________

Word Bank

Cabinet
Clay
executed
free
Missouri
Monroe
revolt
sectional
Seminole
Spanish

Name Date Period

Leaders in the 1820s

Directions The statements below might have been made by important leaders in the 1820s. Decide who may have made each statement. After each statement, write *JM* for James Monroe, *JQA* for John Quincy Adams, *HC* for Henry Clay, or *AJ* for Andrew Jackson.

JM	James Monroe
JQA	John Quincy Adams
HC	Henry Clay
AJ	Andrew Jackson

1. "My military successes will help me win the election." __________
2. "Do I have experience? Why, I have been Speaker of the House." __________
3. "European countries caused problems during my presidency." __________
4. "Gentleman, Great Britain has a proposal for us." __________
5. "Mr. President, I do not agree with the British foreign secretary." __________
6. "I will present the doctrine to Congress." __________
7. "Let me remind you that my father was president." __________
8. "Henry Clay doesn't like my political ideas." __________
9. "We must all support Adams for president." __________
10. "I would like Henry Clay to be my secretary of state." __________

Name Date Period

John Q. Adams and Andrew Jackson

Directions Write the answers to these questions. Use complete sentences.

1. Why was John Quincy Adams not a popular president?

2. Which region of the country did not like the tariff system? Why?

3. What three things happened after the Tariff of 1828 was passed?

4. What is meant by the spoils system?

5. What did Andrew Jackson consider to be his duty as president?

Southern Tension

Directions Write the correct word from the Word Bank to complete each sentence.

Word Bank	
difficult	nullified
higher	opposed
innocent	oppression
lowered	revolt
Nat Turner	unity

1. In 1831, ______________________ and his followers killed slave owners in Virginia.

2. As a result of their ______________________, Nat Turner and about 20 others were hanged.

3. After the rebellion, many ______________________ slaves were killed by fearful owners.

4. Slaves gained the courage to fight ______________________ by whatever means necessary.

5. The South and West ______________________ the tariff act passed in 1828.

6. Northern manufacturers wanted even ______________________ taxes on imports so people would buy their goods.

7. John C. Calhoun, a southerner and Andrew Jackson's vice president, was in a(n) ______________________ position.

8. A new tariff act passed in 1832 ______________________ some tariffs, but neither the North nor South was pleased.

9. South Carolina passed an ordinance that ______________________ tariffs in their state.

10. President Andrew Jackson said that no state would be allowed to challenge the country's ______________________.

Name Date Period

Issues During Jackson's Presidency

Directions The statements below might have been made by people during Andrew Jackson's presidency. Decide who could have said each one. After each statement, write *C* for Congressman, *AI* for American Indian, *AJ* for Andrew Jackson, or *HC* for Henry Clay.

C Congressman
AI American Indian
AJ Andrew Jackson
HC Henry Clay

1. "I'm going to make Jackson's veto an election issue." __________
2. "Gentlemen, we must decrease the fighting between settlers and American Indians." __________
3. "The election of 1832 was a crushing defeat for me." __________
4. "Many of my people died on our journey west." __________
5. "The president vetoed our bill to renew the charter of the Bank." __________
6. "The rich are the only ones that benefit from the Bank." __________
7. "We were not U.S. citizens and were forced out of our homes." __________
8. "In my speeches, I will defend the renewal of the national bank's charter." __________
9. "Before me, presidents almost never used the veto." __________
10. "I am honored to be the National Republican candidate for president." __________
11. "We voted to pass the Indian Removal Act of 1830." __________
12. "We must give the American Indians the land west of the Mississippi River." __________
13. "We were able to keep our home in Florida." __________
14. "I was confident I would win. I didn't think I would lose by so many votes." __________
15. "I support both the common people and the interests of slave owners." __________

Name _______________ Date _______ Period _______

Facts About Texan Independence

Directions Match the words in Column 1 with the details in Column 2. Write the letter on the line.

Column 1

_______ **1.** John Quincy Adams
_______ **2.** Mexico
_______ **3.** William Travis
_______ **4.** Jim Bowie
_______ **5.** Antonio López de Santa Anna
_______ **6.** Alamo
_______ **7.** Goliad
_______ **8.** San Jacinto
_______ **9.** Sam Houston
_______ **10.** Republic of Texas
_______ **11.** Andrew Jackson
_______ **12.** mission
_______ **13.** "Remember the Alamo!"
_______ **14.** Texans
_______ **15.** San Antonio

Column 2

A river near the Gulf of Mexico
B offered Mexico $5 million for Texas
C commander of the Texan army
D refused to sell Texas
E town near the Alamo
F refused to obey Mexican laws
G Texan battle cry
H offered Mexico $1 million for Texas
I Mexican dictator
J church
K Texan colonel at the Alamo
L town in south Texas where Santa Anna won a battle
M rebuilt mission
N famous westerner who died at the Alamo
O Sam Houston became its president

Name Date Period

Workbook Activity
Chapter 11, Lesson 5
49

The Election of 1836

Directions Use the words in the Word Bank to complete the paragraphs. Write each word on the correct line.

Word Bank		
approach	depression	manufacturers
banks	factories	president
careless	farm products	roads
central government	gold or silver	three
charter	loans	unemployment

In the election of 1836, Whig candidates received support from northeastern **1.** ______________________. Their party favored the renewal of the national bank's **2.** ______________________, high tariffs, and a strong **3.** ______________________. Martin Van Buren told voters that a vote for him was like a vote for Jackson because he believed in the same **4.** ______________________. Van Buren got more votes than all **5.** ______________________ Whig candidates together.

Shortly after President Van Buren took office, the country entered a(n) **6.** ______________________, called the Panic of 1837. A good number of small banks had become **7.** ______________________. They used paper money that was not backed by **8.** ______________________. Some had given **9.** ______________________ that were never paid back. When word of these problems got out, many people rushed to their **10.** ______________________ to take out money deposited earlier.

As a result of the panic, many **11.** ______________________ closed. The prices of **12.** ______________________ and manufactured goods fell. New construction of **13.** ______________________ stopped. During this depression, which lasted several years, **14.** ______________________ spread. The **15.** ______________________ was unable to solve many of these problems.

Name Date Period

Workbook Activity **50**
Chapter 12, Lesson 1

How Industry Developed

Directions Write the answers to these questions. Use complete sentences.

1. Between 1790 and 1840, what percentage of Americans lived in rural areas?

____

____

____

2. Why were bankers not eager to lend money to manufacturers?

____

____

____

3. Why did workers form labor unions?

____

____

____

4. Why is Samuel Slater known as "The Father of American Industry"?

____

____

____

5. What advantage did steel plows offer over wooden plows?

____

____

____

Name Date Period

Workbook Activity 51
Chapter 12, Lesson 2

Transportation and Communication Crossword

Directions Read each clue. Then choose the correct word from the Word Bank to complete the puzzle.

Word Bank
canal
commerce
Cumberland
Erie
Field
Fulton
locomotive
Morse
New York
pony express
railroads
steamboats
time
turnpike
west

Across

2. buying or selling goods

4. postal system used for only 18 months

6. what travelers saved with faster transportation

9. carried people up and down the Mississippi River

10. person who laid underwater telegraph cable

14. most important improvement in transportation

15. road travelers paid to use

Down

1. 600-mile road to the West

3. direction canals and railroads took manufactured goods

5. strongest shipping and trading center in the country

7. person who developed the telegraph

8. engine that rides on rails

11. person who traveled by steamboat in 1807

12. name of canal that went from Albany to Buffalo

13. human-made waterway

Name Date Period

Immigrant Facts

Directions Each fact in the Answer Bank describes immigrants from Germany and Ireland. Some facts apply to both groups of immigrants. Write each fact under the correct heading below.

Answer Bank

- By 1850, one million lived in America.
- They left their homeland due to a crop disease.
- By 1850, four million lived in America.
- They escaped political problems in their homeland.
- They became part of the American melting pot.
- They depended on potatoes for food in their homeland.
- They faced starvation in their homeland.
- They hoped for a better life in America.
- Their homeland also had a crop failure, though it was less serious.
- Many settled in American cities.

German Immigrants	Irish Immigrants	Both

Name Date Period

Early Education

Directions Write the correct word from the Word Bank to complete each sentence.

Word Bank

academies	reference book
democracy	standard
education	taxes
grammar	tutors
public	vote

1. Many wealthy families paid ______________________ to teach their children.

2. Some older children attended ______________________ and colleges.

3. ______________________ education was not a popular idea, especially with working-class families.

4. People began to realize that education was important so people could

______________________ wisely.

5. Thomas Jefferson had said that a(n) ______________________ calls for an educated people.

6. In Massachusetts, schools were supported by state ______________________.

7. Horace Mann was in charge of ______________________ for the state of Massachusetts.

8. Noah Webster wrote a series of readers, spellers, and ______________________ books.

9. Webster's books provided a(n) ______________________ of learning for American schoolchildren.

10. A(n) ______________________ is a book used to find information.

Name Date Period

Workbook Activity 54
Chapter 12, Lesson 5

Early American Writers

Directions The statements below might have been made by famous writers during the 1800s. Decide who may have said each one. After each statement, write *EAP* for Edgar Allan Poe, *FD* for Frederick Douglass, *HBS* for Harriet Beecher Stowe, *HWL* for Henry Wadsworth Longfellow, *JFC* for James Fenimore Cooper, or *JGW* for John Greenleaf Whittier.

EAP	Edgar Allan Poe
FD	Frederick Douglass
HBS	Harriet Beecher Stowe
HWL	Henry Wadsworth Longfellow
JFC	James Fenimore Cooper
JGW	John Greenleaf Whittier

1. "Oh, yes, I will give a speech, if that will help people realize the evils of slavery." __________

2. "Our country's history is full of great adventure stories." __________

3. "Please come to the next meeting of the Anti-Slavery Society." __________

4. "I like to think that my book helped end slavery." __________

5. "My newspaper shows my point of view." __________

6. "I have scared my readers out of their wits." __________

7. "I've been attacked by people who support slavery." __________

8. "Could I interest you in a copy of *The North Star*?" __________

9. "It pleases me that you liked the *Leatherstocking Tales*." __________

10. "My most famous poem may be "The Raven." __________

11. "If you are interested in the French and Indian War, I have written something for you." __________

12. "I never went to school—I taught myself all I need to know." __________

13. "I've written poetry and prose about current events." __________

14. "Thousands of copies of my book were sold after it was released in 1852." __________

15. "My poem gives readers a look at that famous ride at the beginning of the Revolutionary War." __________

Early 1840s Timeline

Directions Write the correct name from the Word Bank to complete each sentence in the boxes. Some names will be used more than once.

Word Bank

- Daniel Webster
- Henry Clay
- James K. Polk
- John Tyler
- Martin Van Buren
- William Henry Harrison

1840

In the 1840 election, the Whig candidate is **1.** ____________________ and the Democratic candidate is **2.** ____________________. **3.** ____________________ wins, becoming president in 1841.

1841

President **4.** ____________________ dies and **5.** ____________________ becomes president.

1842

Great Britain and the U.S. dispute the boundary between Maine and Canada. U.S. Secretary of State **6.** ____________________ meets with British Lord Ashburton. They agree on a compromise.

1843

1844

In the 1844 election, the Whig candidate is **7.** ____________________ and the Democratic candidate is **8.** ____________________. **9.** ____________________ wins, becoming president in 1845.

1845

1846

Great Britain and the U.S. dispute the boundary of American Oregon. President **10.** ____________________ and the British sign a treaty that settles the dispute.

Name Date Period

Workbook Activity 56
Chapter 13, Lesson 2

Events in the Mexican War

Directions Put the events in order. Write 1 on the line beside the event that happened first. Write 2 beside the event that happened second. Continue to 15.

_______ **1.** In turn, the United States agreed to pay Mexico $15 million for California and the land between California and Texas.

_______ **2.** Santa Anna surrendered to Sam Houston in the War of Texas Independence.

_______ **3.** Mexican troops crossed the Rio Grande and attacked Taylor's soldiers.

_______ **4.** President Polk sent John Slidell to Mexico City.

_______ **5.** The Mexican officials refused to see John Slidell.

_______ **6.** The United States stretched from coast to coast.

_______ **7.** Santa Anna agreed to turn over land and reset the Texas boundary at the Rio Grande.

_______ **8.** General Zachary Taylor advanced his army beyond the Nueces River.

_______ **9.** President Polk ordered American troops to invade California.

_______ **10.** Nicholas P. Trist went to Mexico to negotiate a treaty.

_______ **11.** General Winfield Scott led a charge on Mexico City.

_______ **12.** The United States declared war with Mexico.

_______ **13.** The Americans captured Mexico City.

_______ **14.** Congress approved the Treaty of Guadalupe Hidalgo.

_______ **15.** Santa Anna said the boundary between Mexico and Texas was the Nueces River.

An Election and the Gold Rush

Directions Write the answers to these questions. Use complete sentences.

1. What were three of President Polk's goals?

2. How did slavery affect the election of 1848?

3. Who was John A. Sutter?

4. Who were the Forty-Niners?

5. What changes did the gold rush bring to California?

Debating Slavery

Directions Write the answers to these questions. Use complete sentences.

1. What did Southerners feel abolitionists were doing?

____

____

____

2. What problem was created when California wanted to become a state?

____

____

____

3. How long did Zachary Taylor serve as president?

____

____

____

4. What law made it easier for slave owners to recapture runaway slaves?

____

____

____

5. Why was the Compromise of 1850 better for the North than for the South?

____

____

____

Name Date Period

Slavery Crossword

Directions Read each clue. Then choose the correct word from the Word Bank to complete the puzzle.

Word Bank

conductors
cotton
Douglass
fugitive
Gadsden
network
Pierce
plantations
raw
Southerners
Southwest
stations
Truth
Tubman
Underground

Across

5. Slaves hid in homes called _____ as they escaped northward.

6. The _____ Railroad helped slaves escape.

8. Many _____ did not think that slavery was wrong.

9. James _____ worked out a purchase of land from Mexico in 1853.

10. A _____ of stations helping runaway slaves stretched from the South to the North and into Canada.

12. _____ was an important crop in the South.

15. Crops such as tobacco and cotton were grown on large [WOL].

Down

1. Frederick _____ was a former slave who helped free others.

2. _____ were people who worked the Underground Railroad.

3. Land that became New Mexico and Arizona was previously part of the _____.

4. Franklin _____ became president in 1853.

7. Under the Fugitive Slave Act, the federal government could settle _____ slave cases.

11. Harriet _____ spoke out against slavery.

13. Sojourner _____ also spoke out against slavery.

14. Cotton was an important _____ material for Northern textile industries.

The Kansas-Nebraska Act

Directions Use the words in the Word Bank to complete the paragraphs. Write each word on the correct line.

Word Bank		
conflicts	Northern	slavery
connected	population	sovereignty
covered wagon	produce	tension
Fugitive	routes	territory
Nebraska	ship	traveled

Since California joined the Union, its **1.** ____________________ had grown a good deal. Thousands of people traveled to the West by **2.** ____________________ on a long journey.

The railroads **3.** ____________________ cities throughout the East. Businesses used them to **4.** ____________________ their goods. Farmers were able to bring their **5.** ____________________ to market by railroad. People **6.** ____________________ more safely than ever before. Congress members discussed possible **7.** ____________________ for a coast-to-coast railroad, but they could not agree.

Northerners had to deal with the problem of building a railroad through Nebraska, which was not an organized **8.** ____________________. Stephen Douglas wanted to organize the territories of **9.** ____________________ and Kansas. In a plan called popular **10.** ____________________, the residents of each territory could choose to enter the Union as a slave state or a free state.

Passage of the Kansas-Nebraska Act caused many **11.** ____________________ among political parties. The **12.** ____________________ between slave states and free states continued to grow.

In 1854, Democrats, Free Soilers, and **13.** ____________________ Whigs met and formed the Republican Party. This new party wanted to take a clear stand on **14.** ____________________. The party wanted to repeal the **15.** ____________________ Slave Law and the Kansas-Nebraska Act.

Problems in Kansas

Directions Write the answers to these questions. Use complete sentences.

1. Most of the proslavery settlers who moved to Kansas came from which Southern states?

2. The violence between the proslavery and antislavery groups in the Kansas territory led to what nickname for the area?

3. Who was David Atchison, and what did he do?

4. Who was John Brown, and what did he do?

5. What happened to the government of Kansas after the election?

Name Date Period

Workbook Activity **62**
Chapter 15, Lesson 2

The Issue of Slavery

Directions Circle the letter of the answer that correctly completes each sentence.

1. The Dred Scott Supreme Court decision ruled that slaves were property ________.

A and could be taken anywhere
B only in slave states
C and could sue for their freedom
D in states but not in territories

2. Democrats chose James Buchanan as their candidate because he was ________.

A against slavery **B** for slavery **C** a safe choice **D** optimistic

3. What Representative Preston Brooks did showed that Americans were turning to ________ to settle slavery disputes.

A laws **B** votes **C** compromises **D** violence

4. Although its candidate lost, the ________ Party showed strength in the 1856 election.

A Democratic **B** Republican **C** American **D** Know-Nothing

5. Senator Charles Sumner made a speech against ________.

A immigration **B** Mexico **C** slavery **D** violence

6. John C. Frémont, the Republican candidate in 1856, was a well-known ________.

A explorer **B** inventor **C** statesman **D** Northerner

7. The American Party wanted ________.

A to end slavery **B** more immigrants **C** fewer immigrants **D** to keep slavery

8. In the Dred Scott case, the Supreme Court ruled that the Missouri Compromise ________ the Constitution.

A supported **B** violated **C** should be added to **D** should be removed from

9. Preston Brooks struck ________ several times with a cane.

A Andrew Butler **B** James Buchanan **C** Charles Sumner **D** Dred Scott

10. Dred Scott argued that he should be a free man because ________.

A his owner had died
B he was a U.S. citizen
C he had lived in Missouri
D he had lived in a free territory

Name Date Period

Workbook Activity 63

Chapter 15, Lesson 3

Leaders in the Late 1850s

Directions The statements below describe leaders in the late 1850s. Decide who each one describes. After each statement, write *AL* for Abraham Lincoln, *SD* for Stephen Douglas, *JB* for John Brown, or *REL* for Robert E. Lee.

AL	Abraham Lincoln
SD	Stephen Douglas
JB	John Brown
REL	Robert E. Lee

1. This man was just over five feet tall. __________

2. His men captured John Brown. __________

3. For two years, he had been a member of the House of Representatives. __________

4. His crime was treason. __________

5. People considered him an excellent speaker. __________

6. He debated Stephen Douglas. __________

7. He believed that violence was sometimes necessary. __________

8. Charlestown, Virginia, was the place of his death. __________

9. He was not a good public speaker. __________

10. This debater knew he had made a mistake. __________

11. Slaves, he believed, should be armed against their owners. __________

12. This colonel was sent to Virginia with marines. __________

13. He captured Harper's Ferry. __________

14. People began to call him "Honest Abe." __________

15. He lost a Senate election, but his popularity increased. __________

Name Date Period

Political Parties in the 1860 Election

Directions Each phrase in the Answer Bank describes one of the four political parties in 1860. Write each phrase under the correct heading below.

Answer Bank

- believed that peace required cooperation
- nominated Stephen Douglas
- believed in higher tariffs
- received 18 percent of the vote
- won the election
- nominated John Bell
- said states would not be allowed to leave the Union
- supported popular sovereignty
- supported slavery
- nominated Abraham Lincoln
- nominated John Breckinridge
- said new territories would not have slavery
- made up of former American Party members and Whigs
- received 29 percent of the vote
- received 13 percent of the vote

Northern Democrats	Southern Democrats

Republicans	Constitutional Unionists

A New Southern Government

Directions Write the answers to these questions. Use complete sentences.

1. What plan did President Buchanan have to bring the country back together again?

____

____

____

2. What compromise did Senator John Crittenden suggest for preserving the Union?

____

____

____

3. How did the Southern states go about forming their own government?

____

____

____

4. How did President Buchanan respond to the Fort Sumter situation?

____

____

____

5. What challenges faced President Lincoln when he took office?

____

____

____

Name Date Period

Workbook Activity 66

Chapter 16, Lesson 2

The Confederates Attack Fort Sumter

Directions Match the words in Column 1 with their descriptions in Column 2. Write the letter on the line.

Column 1

_____ **1.** General Beauregard

_____ **2.** Richmond

_____ **3.** General Robert E. Lee

_____ **4.** Union

_____ **5.** General Winfield Scott

_____ **6.** Major Anderson

_____ **7.** Anaconda

_____ **8.** Fort Sumter

_____ **9.** Confederacy

_____ **10.** defense

_____ **11.** Northern strength

_____ **12.** Southern strength

_____ **13.** forming a blockade

_____ **14.** Virginia

_____ **15.** letting the enemy come

Column 2

A had 11 states

B first commander of the Union army

C name of General Scott's war plan

D Union leader at Fort Sumter

E Confederate commander of South Carolina

F new Confederate capital

G line of defense for the rest of the Confederacy

H part of the Confederate's war plan

I site of the first Civil War attack

J Confederate general known for being an excellent leader

K excellent military leaders

L part of the Union's war plan

M protection against attack

N had 23 states

O most of the country's factories

Civil War Crossword

Directions Read each clue. Then choose the correct word from the Word Bank to complete the puzzle.

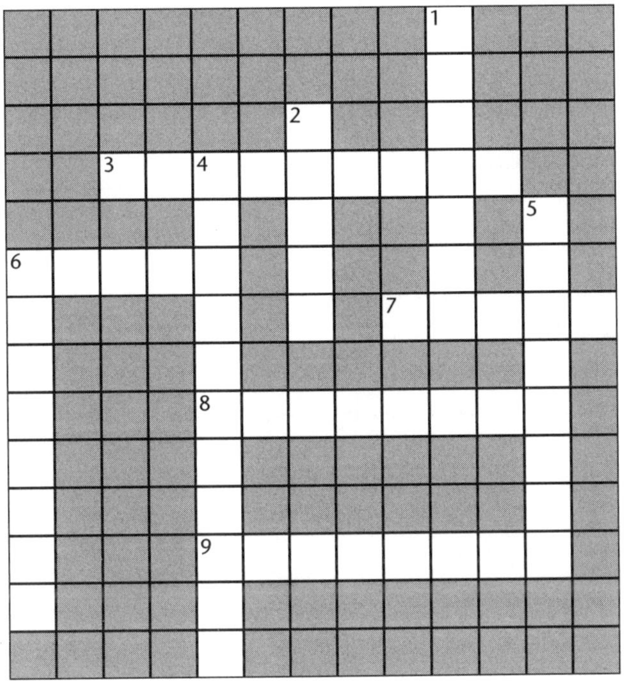

Word Bank

Bull Run
ironclad
Merrimac
outnumbered
Richmond
Scott
Seven
soldiers
Stonewall
Union

Across

3. Confederate General Thomas Jackson's nickname was ______.

6. ______ retired at age 75 and was replaced by George McClellan.

7. The ______ captured two western forts and controlled most of the Mississippi River.

8. The USS ______ was raised and renamed *Virginia.*

9. After the Union's first loss, Northern headlines read, "Forward to ______!"

Down

1. Two separate battles were fought at ______, also called Manassas.

2. The Confederates won the ______ Days Battle near Richmond.

4. McClellan retreated when he knew his army was ______.

5. Two ______ ships fought a battle in 1862, but neither won.

6. More than 12,000 Union ______ died in the Battle of Fredericksburg.

Name Date Period

The Civil War Continues

Directions Each statement in the Answer Bank describes the Union or the Confederacy. Write each statement under the correct heading below.

Answer Bank

- They did not think Abraham Lincoln would free their slaves.
- They were led by Joseph Hooker at Chancellorsville.
- They won at Gettysburg.
- At first, they planned a defensive war.
- George Meade led 85,000 of their soldiers at Gettysburg.
- Their leader thought a major victory in the North would end the war.
- They had 180,000 former slaves in their army.
- They were led by Robert E. Lee in a retreat to the Potomac River.
- These men wounded Stonewall Jackson.
- They lost to a smaller army at Chancellorsville.

Union	Confederacy

Name the General

Directions The statements below might have been made by Ulysses S. Grant, Robert E. Lee, or William Sherman. Decide which general could have said each one. After each statement, write *G* for Grant, *L* for Lee, or *S* for Sherman.

G Ullysses S. Grant
L Robert E. Lee
S William Sherman

1. "I have victories at Shiloh, Perryville, and Murfreesboro." __________

2. "It is unfortunate that we have lost Vicksburg to the Union." __________

3. "I am now commander in chief of all the Union armies." __________

4. "You must destroy everything in sight!" __________

5. "I hope President Lincoln is not re-elected." __________

6. "I ordered General Sherman to attack Atlanta, Georgia." __________

7. "In December 1864, my troops captured Savannah." __________

8. "My troops were surrounded near Appomattox Court House." __________

9. "I will surrender so that no more men will die." __________

10. "You and your soldiers can keep your horses and mules." __________

Reconstruction Plans and Problems

Directions Write the answers to these questions. Use complete sentences.

1. Under President Lincoln's plan, how could a state rejoin the Union?

2. Who shot President Lincoln? Why?

3. What were three problems that faced the Southern states after the Civil War?

4. What was a problem for President Johnson in dealing with Congress?

5. What were the Black Codes?

Name Date Period

Rebuilding the South

Directions Match the words in Column 1 with the details in Column 2. Write the letter on the line.

Column 1

_______ **1.** Tenure of Office Act

_______ **2.** Second Great Removal

_______ **3.** Southern whites

_______ **4.** American Indians

_______ **5.** Edwin Stanton

_______ **6.** Senate

_______ **7.** African Americans

_______ **8.** Radical Republicans

_______ **9.** House of Representatives

_______ **10.** Tennessee

_______ **11.** Civil Rights Act of 1866

_______ **12.** Freedmen's Bureau

_______ **13.** Ulysses S. Grant

_______ **14.** Horatio Seymour

_______ **15.** Reconstruction acts of 1867

Column 2

A voted for Ulysses S. Grant; became important in elections

B quickly accepted the 14th Amendment

C won the 1868 election in a close popular vote

D voted to impeach President Johnson

E was meant to reverse the Black Codes

F blamed Republicans for the Civil War

G put 10 states under military rule

H required Senate approval before a president could fire someone

I held a trial to make a final impeachment ruling

J relocated many American Indians

K fired by President Johnson

L lost the 1868 presidential election

M were not covered by the 14th Amendment

N got many bills passed in Congress

O formed to help former slaves

Name Date Period

Workbook Activity 72
Chapter 17, Lesson 3

Changes in the South

Directions Read each clue. Then choose the correct word from the Word Bank to complete the puzzle.

Word Bank

- carpetbaggers
- coal
- corruption
- cotton
- rights
- scalawags
- segregated
- sharecroppers
- slaves
- tenant

Across

2. After the war, women demanded _____ that had been denied to them.

3. Many small pieces of plantations were rented to _____ farmers.

6. _____ remained a major crop in the South.

8. _____ were Northerners who were elected to political office in the South.

9. Many former _____ became sharecroppers.

10. The discovery of iron ore, limestone, and _____ helped develop the steel industry.

Down

1. Landowners took a large part of the crops of _____.

4. Carpetbaggers often made money through _____.

5. Public schools were _____, with white children attending different schools than African American children.

7. White Southerners who controlled African American politicians were called _____.

Name Date Period

The End of Reconstruction

Directions Use the words in the Word Bank to complete the paragraphs. Write each word on the correct line.

Word Bank

carpetbaggers	depression	outcome	rich	suffrage
clauses	equality	prevented	scalawags	taxes
conditions	murder	Reconstruction	scandals	troops

The 15th Amendment guaranteed **1.** ____________________ to all male citizens. Southerners feared that African Americans would be able to decide the **2.** ____________________ of an election. In some states, African Americans were **3.** ____________________ from voting. Some states passed laws with grandfather **4.** ____________________ that made many African Americans unable to vote.

The Ku Klux Klan wanted to make **5.** ____________________ leave the South. They also wanted to punish the **6.** ____________________. The violence of the Klan, while intended to scare victims, often led to **7.** ____________________.

President Grant's administration was harmed by many **8.** ____________________. Many of the friends he appointed to government positions tried to get **9.** ____________________ through their power in government. During Grant's second term in office, the country went into a **10.** ____________________.

After 10 years of Reconstruction, Northerners grew tired of it. They disliked the high **11.** ____________________, and they felt it was time for the South to take care of itself. Rutherford B. Hayes told Southern Democratic leaders he would end **12.** ____________________ if they would support him as president. Shortly after, he took office. Hayes had all federal **13.** ____________________ removed from the South.

Southern state governments denied African Americans social **14.** ____________________ and the right to vote. In many cases, **15.** ____________________ for African Americans were not much better than they had been before the Civil War.

Name Date Period

Workbook Activity
Chapter 18, Lesson 1
74

Railroad Review

Directions Write the answers to these questions. Use complete sentences.

1. What form of transportation did most Americans use to travel to the West before the completion of the transcontinental railroad?

____

____

____

2. Before the transcontinental railroad was completed, how were goods and supplies shipped from east to west?

____

____

____

3. What improved communication in 1861?

____

____

____

4. What two companies were chosen to build the transcontinental railroad? Where did each company begin construction?

____

____

____

5. Where did the two railroads meet? How was the completion of the transcontinental railroad celebrated?

____

____

____

Name Date Period

Miners, Cowhands, and Farmers

Directions Write each word or phrase from the Word Bank under the correct heading.

Word Bank		
branding	longhorn cattle	shovels, picks, and pans
Chisholm Trail	Nevada	sod houses
dry farming	Pikes Peak	stampedes
gold and silver	prospectors	Texas
homesteaders	railroad holding pens	windmills

Miners

1. ______________________
2. ______________________
3. ______________________
4. ______________________
5. ______________________

Cowhands

6. ______________________
7. ______________________
8. ______________________
9. ______________________
10. ______________________
11. ______________________

Farmers

12. ______________________
13. ______________________
14. ______________________
15. ______________________

Name Date Period

Workbook Activity 76

Chapter 18, Lesson 3

Plains Indians Crossword

Directions Read each clue. Then choose the correct word from the Word Bank to complete the puzzle.

Word Bank

- buffalo
- Cheyenne
- Cloud
- Cody
- Custer
- Dakota
- Horn
- horse
- Montana
- Nez Percé
- prospectors
- reservations
- Sioux
- Sitting
- Spirit

Across

3. By 1889, there were only 541 ______ in the country.

6. The ______ and Sioux defended their lands against the Seventh Cavalry.

8. American Indians believed the Great ______ lived in the Black Hills.

9. Once gold was discovered in the Black Hills, ______ could not be kept away.

13. Custer's Last Stand occurred at the Little Big ______ River in 1876.

14. The Plains Indians won a major battle against Colonel Custer in the state of ______.

15. Chief Red ______ spoke in Washington, D.C., about the government's broken promises.

Down

1. Chief Crazy ______ helped gather 2,000 warriors to fight.

2. George Armstrong ______ led the Seventh Cavalry and died with his men.

4. Government officials wanted to kill the buffalo and put the Plains Indians on ______.

5. The Black Hills were holy to the ______.

7. Chief Joseph led the ______ toward Canada to avoid more bloodshed.

10. Chief ______ Bull helped lead a large Indian force to victory.

11. William F. ______ got the name "Buffalo Bill" after he killed thousands of buffalo.

12. By the mid-1870s, there were reservations in New Mexico, Arizona, and the territories of ______ and Wyoming.

Name Date Period

Workbook Activity

Chapter 18, Lesson 4

77

Failed Attempts to Help American Indians

Directions Write the correct phrase from the Answer Bank to complete each sentence.

Answer Bank

- no frontier line
- the western lands
- had been mistreated
- every member of Congress
- family-size farms
- religion
- their old way of life
- by government agents
- become independent farmers
- killed or wounded

1. *A Century of Dishonor* told how badly American Indians

____

2. Helen Hunt Jackson's book was given to

____

3. The Dawes Severalty Act was intended to help American Indians

____

4. American Indian lands were divided into

____

5. Sometimes, American Indians were taken advantage of

____

6. The Ghost Dance was a

____

7. Some American Indians hoped the Ghost Dance would bring back

____

8. At Wounded Knee, South Dakota, 290 Ghost Dance followers were

____

9. By 1890, there was

____

10. Between 1864 and 1912, 13 states were created from

____

The Industrial Age

Directions Read each clue. Then choose the correct word from the Word Bank to complete the puzzle.

Word Bank

- Bessemer
- Brooklyn
- Carnegie
- engineering
- entrepreneurs
- generous
- iron
- Kelly
- labor
- petroleum
- resources
- rust
- skyscraper
- steel
- suspension

Across

2. Immigrants gave American industries an eager ______ force.

4. Steel is purified ______.

6. A ten-story building made with steel supports was called a(n) ______.

9. Iron could ______ and was not very strong.

11. New businesses are started and organized by ______.

13. The Brooklyn Bridge is an example of modern ______.

14. Andrew Carnegie learned a method of making ______ in England.

15. Carnegie was ______, giving $350 million in his lifetime.

Down

1. The ______ Bridge was the longest suspension bridge in 1883.

3. Coal, iron, and lumber are natural ______.

5. In England, Henry ______ developed an inexpensive way to make steel.

7. A ______ bridge is supported by wires attached to towers.

8. ______ is a liquid used to make fuel.

10. ______'s company made steel for railroad tracks.

12. William ______, an American, also developed a method for making steel.

Name Date Period

Events in the Development of the Oil Industry

Directions Put each set of events in order. Write *1* on the line beside the event that happened first. Write *2* beside the event that happened second, and so on.

Set 1: Number from 1 to 6.

______ **A** Oil refineries were built.

______ **B** Most people believed that oil was not very valuable.

______ **C** Drake drilled the first oil well in 1859.

______ **D** Edwin Drake went to Titusville, Pennsylvania.

______ **E** A scientist said that rock oil could be made into lamp fuel.

______ **F** Oil prospectors went to Titusville and built oil wells.

Set 2: Number from 1 to 5.

______ **G** Rockefeller thought that drilling for oil was risky.

______ **H** The Standard Oil Company controlled the production and price of U.S. oil.

______ **I** He created the Standard Oil Company of Ohio in 1870.

______ **J** John D. Rockefeller went to Titusville.

______ **K** He decided to refine the oil instead.

Set 3: Number from 1 to 4.

______ **L** The need for kerosene lamps ended.

______ **M** The motor car created a new use for oil: gasoline.

______ **N** The indoor electric light was invented.

______ **O** Most oil was used for kerosene in lamps.

Inventors and Industry Leaders

Directions Match the names in Column 1 with the details in Column 2. Write the letter on the line.

Column 1

_____ **1.** Alexander Graham Bell

_____ **2.** Thomas Alva Edison

_____ **3.** George Eastman

_____ **4.** Ottmar Mergenthaler

_____ **5.** Elisha Otis

_____ **6.** Henry Ford

_____ **7.** Gustavus Swift

_____ **8.** James J. Hill

_____ **9.** Cornelius Vanderbilt

_____ **10.** Theodore Roosevelt

Column 2

A invented a typesetting machine

B was called the Wizard of Menlo Park

C created America's first great railroad system, the New York Central

D developed an assembly line method for building cars

E invented the telephone

F started conservation programs

G developed the Great Northern Railway System

H simplified the Kodak camera

I helped develop the meatpacking industry in midwestern cities

J invented the elevator

Name Date Period

Workbook Activity 81

Chapter 20, Lesson 1

Cities and Factories

Directions Write the answers to these questions. Use complete sentences.

1. In 1850, what percentage of the U.S. population lived in cities? By 1900, what was this percentage?

____

____

____

2. Where were factories usually built?

____

____

____

3. What lowered the cost of products?

____

____

____

4. How much money did many factory employees earn in a week?

____

____

____

5. Why could employers pay such low wages to factory workers?

____

____

____

Name Date Period

Workbook Activity 82
Chapter 20, Lesson 2

Immigration and Discrimination

Directions Read each clue. Then choose the correct word from the Word Bank to complete the puzzle.

Word Bank

- Chinese
- discrimination
- equal
- Homestead
- immigrants
- Italy
- Jim Crow
- Jewish
- Liberty
- Louisiana
- Plessy
- prejudice
- race
- segregation
- Supreme

Across

2. ______ Laws separated African Americans and whites.

5. The ______ Court ruled that the 14th Amendment applied to state governments and not individuals.

9. The ______ Act of 1862 offered cheap farmland to immigrants.

11. The Statue of ______ was a gift from France in 1884.

12. ______ passed a law requiring railroad companies to have segregated facilities.

13. In 1882, Congress passed a law that prevented ______ immigrants from entering the country.

14. Homer ______ challenged segregation in a court case and lost.

Down

1. African Americans were treated unfairly because of their ______.

2. During the 1880s, almost half of Polish and Russian immigrants were ______.

3. Many immigrants left eastern Europe to escape religious ______.

4. Many new immigrants experienced ______ in America.

6. The Civil Rights Act of 1875 had made ______ in public places illegal.

7. The largest group of new immigrants came from ______.

8. Most ______ were very poor, worked hard jobs, and could not speak English.

10. The Supreme Court said that "separate but ______" facilities were constitutional.

City Living

Directions Use the words in the Word Bank to complete the paragraphs. Write each word on the correct line.

Word Bank				
basketball	fixed	museums	retail	spectator
department	income	Naismith	schedule	streetcars
electric	leisure	orchestras	specialized	trolleys

Many American cities had theaters, music halls, skating rinks, and other **1.** ____________________ activities. Libraries offered the opportunity to read books. **2.** ____________________ areas included stores and restaurants.

City transportation included horse-drawn **3.** ____________________ that carried 10 to 15 people at a time. After the **4.** ____________________ motor was invented, people traveled in larger vehicles known as **5.** ____________________. These were inexpensive to ride, and they ran on a set time **6.** ____________________.

The early stores **7.** ____________________ in a few products. Shoppers went from one store to another. Then business owners put many different stores into one large building. These **8.** ____________________ stores became very popular. F. W. Woolworth was one of the first to offer many different products at a **9.** ____________________ price. People who lived on a limited **10.** ____________________ were able to buy many items for a small amount of money.

Many cities built opera houses and halls for symphony **11.** ____________________. Works of art could be seen at public **12.** ____________________. Sports teams were organized. Baseball became a favorite **13.** ____________________ sport in the summer. James **14.** ____________________ invented a winter sport known as **15.** ____________________.

Name Date Period

City Problems

Directions Read each statement. Choose the best meaning for each underlined word or phrase from the Answer Bank. Write the meaning on the line.

Word Bank

city
dangerous
immigrants
skills
slums
tenements
ventilation
waste disposal
Young Men's Christian Association
Young Women's Christian Association

1. With the large numbers of people in many cities, sanitation was poor. __________

2. The lack of fire escapes made tenements unsafe places to live. __________

3. The YMCA helped the urban poor. __________

4. Many families lived together in cheaply made apartment buildings. __________

5. The YWCA also helped the urban poor. __________

6. Jacob Riis wrote about the living conditions of people who had moved from other countries. __________

7. Many people had to live close together in urban areas with poor living conditions. __________

8. Some of the buildings had little circulating fresh air in them. __________

9. Some people believed that the poor were lazy or had no ability to do things. __________

10. Urban leaders were not sure how to deal with many of the problems. __________

Name Date Period

Scandals and More Scandals

Directions Write the answers to these questions. Use complete sentences.

1. Why did Mark Twain use the term "Gilded Age" as a label for the 1870s?

2. What feeling did reform leaders have about industrial leaders?

3. At first, how did Crédit Mobilier's activities affect its stock?

4. What did William Belknap do that showed he was corrupt?

5. What happened in the Whisky Ring Scandal?

Political Reforms Puzzle

Directions Read each clue. Then choose the correct word from the Word Bank to complete the puzzle.

Word Bank
Arthur
boss
bribe
civil
Cleveland
corruption
fees
Garfield
Hayes
Nast
political
railroad
reforms
spoils
Tweed

Across

1. President Arthur had many ______ enemies and was not nominated for re-election.
6. Newspapers criticized government ______.
7. The Interstate Commerce Act forced railroad companies to charge fair ______.
9. Mugwumps and other groups wanted many ______.
10. A(n) ______ is a payment to make a person act in a certain way.
12. Reformers worked to put President ______ in office.
13. Boss ______ stole city money and was convicted in 1873.
14. President ______ fired federal workers who got paid without doing work.

Down

2. Mugwumps wanted a(n) ______ service system.
3. William Tweed was a powerful ______ in New York City.
4. President ______ convinced Congress to pass civil service laws.
5. The ______ system allowed friends of politicians to get government jobs.
8. Charles Guiteau shot President ______ because he didn't get a government job.
9. The ______ companies did not want the government to regulate their business.
11. Thomas ______ drew political cartoons that brought attention to corruption.

Name ______________________ Date ________ Period ________

Workbook Activity 87
Chapter 21, Lesson 3

Labor Unions

Directions Use the words in the Word Bank to complete the paragraphs. Write each word on the correct line.

Word Bank		
all	Knights of Labor	strikes
Chicago	membership	strikebreakers
demands	peaceful bargaining	Terrence Powderly
eight-hour	Samuel Gompers	Uriah Stevens
Haymarket Square	secret	workers

In 1869, **1.** ______________________ organized the Noble Order of the Knights of Labor. This union was small. It was also a **2.** ______________________ organization. Ten years later, a new leader named **3.** ______________________ changed the union. The union accepted **4.** ______________________ workers, including women and blacks. Its membership grew rapidly.

In 1886, the American Federation of Labor was formed. Its leader was **5.** ______________________. This new union organized many different groups of skilled **6.** ______________________ into one powerful union. The AFL favored **7.** ______________________, while the Knights of Labor favored **8.** ______________________ and boycotts.

To strike a company, union workers refused to work until their **9.** ______________________ were met. Companies sometimes hired new workers to replace the strikers. These nonunion workers were called **10.** ______________________. Sometimes violence would occur when strikebreakers tried to take the jobs of union workers.

One instance of violence occurred at **11.** ______________________ in the city of **12.** ______________________. Workers were on strike to gain a(n) **13.** ______________________ workday. At a protest meeting, a bomb was thrown. Several people were killed. Many people blamed the **14.** ______________________ for this. As a result, the union's **15.** ______________________ steadily declined.

Name Date Period

Workbook Activity 88
Chapter 21, Lesson 4

The Populist Party

Directions Each detail in the Answer Bank was believed to help either big business or the average American in the 1880s. Write each detail under the correct heading below.

Answer Bank

- farm alliances
- gold standard
- graduated income tax
- Grover Cleveland
- higher crop prices
- Interstate Commerce Commission
- James Weaver
- limited money supply
- Populist Party
- publicly owned railroads
- Sherman Antitrust Act
- silver coins
- trust companies
- William Jennings Bryan
- William McKinley

Big Business

1. __________

2. __________

3. __________

4. __________

5. __________

Average American

6. __________

7. __________

8. __________

9. __________

10. __________

11. __________

12. __________

13. __________

14. __________

15. __________

Problems with Spain

Directions Write the answers to these questions. Use complete sentences.

1. What helped put America in a better position to compete with the countries of Europe?

2. What parts of the former Spanish empire remained in North America?

3. Why was America so concerned about Cuba?

4. What did President McKinley offer to avoid a war with Spain? How did Spain respond?

5. Why did Theodore Roosevelt send an American fleet to the Philippines?

Name Date Period

The Splendid Little War

Directions Each statement in the Answer Bank refers to either Cuba or the Philippines. Write each statement under the correct heading below.

Answer Bank

- Admiral Dewey destroyed the Spanish navy there.
- The Rough Riders captured San Juan Hill there.
- It is in the Caribbean Sea.
- The United States withdrew in 1902, after an agreement with it.
- The United States paid Spain $20 million for it.
- It is in the Pacific Ocean.
- The United States improved its education and sanitation.
- Its people did not want to belong to the United States.
- The U.S. Army was sent to stop its fight for independence.
- A valuable U.S. naval base was established there.
- American forces remained there for four years.
- Admiral Sampson sank Spanish ships there.
- The United States fought its army for three years.
- Walter Reed rid it of yellow fever.

Cuba	The Philippines
1.	**8.**
2.	**9.**
3.	**10.**
4.	**11.**
5.	**12.**
6.	**13.**
7.	**14.**

The United States and China

Directions Match the words in Column 1 with the details in Column 2. Write the letter on the line.

	Column 1		Column 2
______ **1.**	foreigners	**A**	U.S. Secretary of State
______ **2.**	Open Door Policy	**B**	people from another country
______ **3.**	Hawaiian Islands	**C**	Chinese who rebelled
______ **4.**	John Hay	**D**	American trading plan for China
______ **5.**	Japan	**E**	ocean between China and the United States
______ **6.**	American universities	**F**	formed to discuss removing foreigners from China
______ **7.**	European countries	**G**	Asian country that gained Chinese land
______ **8.**	Boxers	**H**	maintained a friendly relationship with China
______ **9.**	China's trade	**I**	money returned was used to send Chinese young people to these
______ **10.**	Pacific	**J**	established their own government and courts in China
______ **11.**	troops	**K**	with Hawaii, gave America a stronger ability to trade with the Far East
______ **12.**	Boxer Rebellion	**L**	became an American territory in 1900
______ **13.**	secret political clubs	**M**	American merchants were afraid it would fall under control of a few countries
______ **14.**	United States	**N**	sent to China to protect American interests
______ **15.**	Philippines	**O**	revolt in China in 1900

Turn-of-the-Century Crossword

Directions Read each clue. Then choose the correct word from the Word Bank to complete the puzzle.

Word Bank

- Bryan
- deal
- imperialism
- initiative
- Labor
- McKinley
- miners
- muckrakers
- primary
- Progressives
- recall
- referendum
- reforms
- Rockefeller
- Roosevelt

Across

2. Ida Tarbell accused ______ of making an oil monopoly.

4. Roosevelt said American workers need a square ______.

5. Progressives wanted voters to have the use of a ______.

7. Roosevelt supported the right of ______ to strike.

9. ______ was the Democratic candidate in the 1900 election.

11. ______ was assassinated shortly after he was re-elected.

12. Progressives thought citizens should suggest a new law with a(n) ______.

13. Republicans avoided the issue of ______ during the 1900 election campaign.

14. ______ wanted to pass laws to fix social and political problems.

Down

1. With a ______, voters can reject or approve bills.

2. ______ became the youngest president when he took office in 1901.

3. The Department of ______ and Commerce watched over big businesses.

6. In a(n) ______ election, people choose the candidates.

8. Upton Sinclair and Lincoln Steffens were ______.

10. Progressive economic ______ were usually most helpful to white workers.

Roosevelt's Accomplishments in Numbers

Directions Write the correct number from the Answer Bank to complete each sentence. One number will be used twice.

Answer Bank		
3	1902	1908
10	1905	1914
150	1906	7,000

1. The Panama Canal was completed in ______________.

2. President Roosevelt helped Russia and Japan end their war in ______________.

3. Congress passed the Meat Inspection Act in ______________.

4. Gifford Pinchot convinced the president to add ______________ million acres of land to the country's forest preserve.

5. The federal government gained the power to build dams and create irrigation projects by a law passed in ______________.

6. Many state governments set up their own conservation projects after a national conference held in ______________.

7. The United States had ______________ foreign policy plans.

8. The Republic of Panama received $ ______________ million from the United States, plus yearly rent.

9. The Panama Canal took ______________ years to build.

10. The Panama Canal cut the shipping distance from New York to San Francisco by more than ______________ miles.

Name _____ Date _____ Period _____

Workbook Activity 94

Chapter 22, Lesson 6

Roosevelt Becomes a Bull Moose

Directions Use the words in the Word Bank to complete the paragraphs. Write each word on the correct line.

Word Bank

16th Amendment	Democratic Party	Republican Party
American society	federal government	Standard Oil Trust
American Tobacco Company	Labor	William Howard Taft
Bull Moose Party	New Freedom	William Jennings Bryan
Commerce	New Nationalism	Woodrow Wilson
Congress		

President Roosevelt, not wanting a third term in office, convinced the **1.** _____________ to nominate **2.** _____________. Their candidate had no trouble winning the presidency. He defeated the **3.** _____________ candidate, **4.** _____________.

President Taft took office in 1909. He demanded a restructuring of the **5.** _____________. He ordered the breakup of the **6.** _____________. During his administration, the government received the power to collect income taxes through the passage of the **7.** _____________. Also, the separate Departments of **8.** _____________ and **9.** _____________ were set up.

In 1912, Roosevelt sought re-election as a candidate of the **10.** _____________. He went against Republican Taft and the Democratic candidate, **11.** _____________. The Democrats had a reform plan called the **12.** _____________, Roosevelt called his program the **13.** _____________. Roosevelt believed the **14.** _____________ should be responsible for regulating big business and improving **15.** _____________.The Democrats won the election.

Name Date Period

Workbook Activity
Chapter 23, Lesson 1
95

The War Begins in Europe

Directions Write the answers to these questions. Use complete sentences.

1. What political experience did Woodrow Wilson have before he became president?

2. What specific event started the war?

3. Explain the chain reaction that occurred when Austria-Hungary declared war on Serbia?

4. Which countries made up the Central Powers?

5. Which countries made up the Allied Powers?

Name Date Period

Workbook Activity 96

Chapter 23, Lesson 2

America's Neutral Policy Is Tested

U	United States
B	Great Britain
G	Germany
F	France

Directions The statements below might have been made by someone from the United States, Great Britain, Germany, or France. Decide which country the speaker most likely belonged to. After each statement, write *U* for the United States, *B* for Great Britain, *G* for Germany, or *F* for France. Some answers will be two letters.

1. "The United States is not acting like a neutral country." __________
2. "We re-elected our president because he kept us out of war." __________
3. "We bought many war supplies from the United States." __________ and __________
4. "The *Lusitania* was carrying war supplies." __________
5. "Our companies can sell war supplies in Europe." __________
6. "We want the United States to stop trading with Great Britain." __________
7. "We helped the United States during their Revolutionary War." __________
8. "We sank the *Lusitania* with a torpedo from a U-boat." __________
9. "The *Lusitania* did not have any war supplies on board." __________
10. "We are part of the Central Powers." __________
11. "We are part of the Allied Powers." __________ and __________
12. "We set up war zones in the Atlantic Ocean." __________ and __________
13. "After the *Lusitania* disaster, we began to turn against Germany." __________
14. "We have the same language and many of the same customs as Americans." __________
15. "Our navy tried to prevent Americans from trading with Germany." __________

World War I Crossword

Directions Read each clue. Then choose the correct word from the Word Bank to complete the puzzle.

Word Bank

- bonds
- consumer
- doughboys
- draft
- France
- Mexico
- peace
- Pershing
- riots
- standstill
- trenches
- U-boats
- Wilson
- women
- Zimmermann

Across

2. Something not changing or improving

6. Country where German and Allied officers met to discuss an armistice

7. Country that was promised land in exchange for help

8. General who led American troops in World War I

10. Goods that factories stopped making so they could make war supplies

11. Items sold by the U.S. government to raise money

13. America's president during the war

14. Ditches that soldiers fought from on the Western Front

Down

1. What the U.S. president wanted for Europe in 1917

3. Nickname for American soldiers fighting in Europe

4. Racial conflicts after African Americans moved to northern cities

5. Secret note released to U.S. newspapers in 1917

9. German submarines

12. Practice of requiring people to serve in the armed forces

13. Those who joined the armed forces as nurses and office workers

Wilson's Plan for Permanent Peace

Directions Match the words in Column 1 with the details in Column 2. Write the letter on the line.

Column 1

_______ **1.** David Lloyd George

_______ **2.** Georges Clemenceau

_______ **3.** Vittorio Orlando

_______ **4.** Wilson's 14 Points

_______ **5.** League of Nations

_______ **6.** "Big Four"

_______ **7.** Treaty of Versailles

_______ **8.** Yugoslavia

_______ **9.** Paris Peace Conference

_______ **10.** Czechoslovakia

Column 2

A meeting whose purpose was to write a peace treaty to end the war

B new nation that included Bosnia and Serbia

C leader of Great Britain at the end of World War I

D leader of Italy at the end of World War I

E leader of France at the end of World War I

F organization that would settle disputes between countries

G one of the new nations created from the Austro-Hungarian Empire

H Wilson's plan for permanent peace

I group of political leaders who went to the Paris Peace Conference

J peace treaty that was not ratified by the U.S. Senate

Name Date Period

Presidents Harding and Coolidge

Directions Write the answers to these questions. Use complete sentences.

1. What was Warren Harding's campaign promise?

____

____

____

2. What percentage of the popular vote did Warren Harding receive in the election of 1920?

____

____

____

3. What event led to Calvin Coolidge becoming president?

____

____

____

4. Why was the Veteran's Bureau established?

____

____

____

5. Why was Secretary of the Interior Albert B. Fall jailed?

____

____

____

Social Changes in the Twenties

Directions Write the correct phrase from the Answer Bank to complete each sentence.

Answer Bank

- 10 million Americans
- 19th Amendment
- assembly line
- became affordable
- challenge old ideas
- commercial radio station
- communication by phone
- leisure time
- monthly payments
- more mobile
- older generation
- right to vote
- social changes
- social freedom
- unlimited source

1. Many ______________________ occurred in America in the 1920s.

2. People's purchasing power changed when they could buy things in ______________________.

3. People were brought closer together through ______________________.

4. Americans had more money and more ______________________.

5. As more people bought cars, American society became ______________________.

6. In the mid-1920s, the price of cars dropped, so they ______________________ to a greater number of people.

7. The Model T was the first car made on a(n) ______________________.

8. The radio became a(n) ______________________ of information and entertainment.

9. In 1920, the first permanent ______________________ began broadcasting.

10. By 1929, about ______________________ owned radios.

11. The National Woman Suffrage Association wanted to give women the ______________________.

12. The ______________________ gave all American women the right to vote.

13. Women of the 1920s refused to be tied down to the ideas of the ______________________.

14. Women began to ______________________ about how they should act.

15. Women's desire to gain more ______________________ could be seen in their style of dress.

Name Date Period

Workbook Activity 101
Chapter 24, Lesson 3

The Jazz Age

Directions Match the words in Column 1 with the descriptions in Column 2. Write the letter on the line.

Column 1

_____ **1.** spiritual

_____ **2.** jazz

_____ **3.** composer

_____ **4.** symphony

_____ **5.** Charleston

_____ **6.** Duke Ellington

_____ **7.** *The Great Gatsby*

_____ **8.** Sinclair Lewis

_____ **9.** Harlem

_____ **10.** John Dos Passos

_____ **11.** Harlem Renaissance

_____ **12.** Langston Hughes

_____ **13.** *The Age of Innocence*

_____ **14.** African Americans

_____ **15.** "Rhapsody in Blue"

Column 2

A African American writer and poet

B writer who described small-town life

C lively style of music that is improvised

D time of great creativity by African American writers

E creators of the jazz style of music

F area of New York City

G religious song

H novel about the foolishness of New York high society

I novel by F. Scott Fitzgerald

J writer of jazz music for big bands

K energetic dance of the 1920s

L long, complex musical piece

M symphony by George Gershwin

N writer who described the sadness of World War I veterans

O someone who writes music

Name Date Period

Workbook Activity **102**
Chapter 24, Lesson 4

Social Problems in the Twenties

Directions Each statement in the Answer Bank is related to the Ku Klux Klan, the Immigration Act, or Prohibition. Write each statement under the correct heading below.

Answer Bank

- The 21st Amendment repealed it.
- Its supporters helped elect governors in two states.
- It was meant to protect U.S. democracy from Communists.
- It limited the number of immigrants from Europe.
- Because of it, the 1920s became known as "The Dry Decade."
- It defined an American as white, Protestant, and native born.
- Bootleggers and speakeasies ignored it.
- It was a reaction to the Russian revolution.
- Its supporters held a parade in Washington, D.C.
- It was brought about by the 18th Amendment.

Ku Klux Klan

1. ______________________________

2. ______________________________

3. ______________________________

Immigration Act

4. ______________________________

5. ______________________________

6. ______________________________

Prohibition

7. ______________________________

8. ______________________________

9. ______________________________

10. ______________________________

The Rise and Fall of American Confidence

Directions Match the items in Column 1 with the details in Column 2. Write the letter on the line.

Column 1

_____ **1.** Herbert Hoover

_____ **2.** Great Depression

_____ **3.** Lucky Lindy, Babe Ruth, and profitable business

_____ **4.** Charles Lindbergh

_____ **5.** Al Smith

_____ **6.** stock market

_____ **7.** profit

_____ **8.** *Spirit of St. Louis*

_____ **9.** soup house

_____ **10.** Radio Corporation of America

_____ **11.** Babe Ruth

_____ **12.** Calvin Coolidge

_____ **13.** Paris, France

_____ **14.** New York

_____ **15.** Roaring Twenties

Column 2

A pilot who made the first solo flight across the Atlantic

B man who hit 60 home runs

C company whose stock increased $400 in one year

D Charles Lindbergh's destination

E Republican candidate in 1928

F president who did not seek re-election in 1928

G city Lindbergh left from

H Democratic candidate in 1928

I what stock buyers hoped to make

J symbols of American confidence and strength

K name for the decade before the Great Depression

L place where the poor got food

M name of Lindbergh's plane

N market for buying and selling stock

O time of great economic struggle in America

Causes of the Great Depression

Directions Write the answers to these questions. Use complete sentences.

1. Why was industrial production slowed after 1930?

2. Why did many banks go out of business during the Great Depression?

3. What were two reasons for the decline in American exports during the 1920s?

4. How did the Dust Bowl affect farmers?

5. How did Americans lose confidence?

Hoover or Roosevelt?

Directions Each plan in the Answer Bank was suggested by either Herbert Hoover or Franklin Roosevelt. Write each one under the correct heading below.

Answer Bank

- The Tennessee Valley Authority put thousands to work on construction projects.
- A moratorium was put on war debts to the United States so that Europe would be able to buy U.S. products.
- The National Recovery Administration was established to help businesses recover.
- The Federal Emergency Relief Administration loaned money to states for food, clothing, and shelter.
- The Emergency Banking Act made federal loans available to banks.
- Congress approved $500 million to buy surplus crops from farmers.
- A federal public works program was set up to create jobs.
- The Reconstruction Finance Corporation was established to lend money to banks, insurance companies, and railroads.
- A national "bank holiday" prevented people from taking all of their money from banks.
- The Civilian Conservation Corps hired young people to plant trees, build roads, and help with flood control.

Herbert Hoover

1. ______________________________

2. ______________________________

3. ______________________________

4. ______________________________

Franklin Roosevelt

5. ______________________________

6. ______________________________

7. ______________________________

8. ______________________________

9. ______________________________

10. ______________________________

New Deal Crossword

Directions Read each clue. Then choose the correct word from the Word Bank to complete the puzzle.

1															
2	3	4	5	6	7	8	9	10	11	12	13	14	15		

Word Bank

aid
collective
Democratic
Housing
Lewis
liberal
murals
nine
occupations
overturn
Owners
Perkins
Security
Wagner
Works

Across

4. In the 1936 election, many union workers, farmers, and African Americans voted for the _______ candidate.

9. _______ bargaining was a peaceful way to negotiate between workers and employers.

13. The CIO united workers who had many different _______.

14. John _______ wanted an industry-wide union that was open to all workers.

15. President Roosevelt did not want the Supreme Court to _______ New Deal laws.

Down

1. The Home _______ Loan Corporation offered low-interest loans.

2. The _______ Act gave workers the right to form unions.

3. _______ from New Deal programs convinced African Americans to vote for Roosevelt.

5. The _______ Progress Administration was part of the Second New Deal stage.

6. President Roosevelt appointed _______ judges who favored change.

7. The Social _______ Act helped the elderly, unemployed, and disabled.

8. Frances _______ was the first woman on a presidential Cabinet.

10. As part of the WPA, artists were hired to paint _______ on buildings.

11. The Federal _______ Administration encouraged home building and repair.

12. After the NRA and AAA were declared unconstitutional, Roosevelt referred to the Supreme Court as the "_______ old men."

Name Date Period

Escape from the Depression

Directions Match the people and places in Column 1 with the descriptions in Column 2. Write the letter on the line.

Column 1

_____ **1.** Fred Astaire

_____ **2.** Marx brothers

_____ **3.** Shirley Temple

_____ **4.** Joe Louis

_____ **5.** Max Schmeling

_____ **6.** Jesse Owens

_____ **7.** Georgia

_____ **8.** Amelia Earhart

_____ **9.** Adolf Hitler

_____ **10.** Berlin, Germany

Column 2

A setting of the movie *Gone With the Wind*

B child star who often played the part of an orphan

C German boxer who lost

D leader of Germany in 1936

E athlete who won four gold medals in the 1936 Olympics

F comedians of the 1930s

G American boxer who won

H popular dance partner of Ginger Rogers

I place where the 1936 Olympics were held

J first woman to fly alone over the Atlantic Ocean

The Rise of the Nazi Party in Germany

Directions Write the answers to these questions. Use complete sentences.

1. What caused the collapse of the German economy in 1923?

2. How did Adolf Hitler become the dictator of Germany?

3. Who did Hitler blame for Germany's problems? How were these people treated?

4. Why did Americans feel safe from foreign attack?

5. What did the neutrality laws of 1935 and 1937 forbid?

Name Date Period

Moving Toward a Second World War

Directions Read each clue. Then choose the correct word from the Word Bank to complete the puzzle.

Word Bank

appeasement
Austria
camps
Czechoslovakia
Danzig
Holocaust
League
Munich
Night
Polish
prime
Reich
Stalin
threat
Treaty

Across

1. The main leaders of Europe met in ________, Germany, in 1938.
5. The British and French leaders agreed to a policy of ________ over the Sudentenland.
7. The Nazis sent millions of Jews by train to death ________.
8. The ________ Corridor divided Germany into two parts.
9. The ________ was the mass murder of European Jews during World War II.
13. Adolf Hitler demanded that Poland give back the city of ________.
14. Hitler's ________ of war frightened Chamberlain and Daladier.

Down

2. The Sudentenland was part of ________.
3. Hitler wanted to establish the Third ________ in Germany.
4. Soviet leader Joseph ________ signed a friendship treaty with Hitler.
5. In 1938, ________ became part of the German empire.
6. Neville Chamberlain was the ________ minister of Great Britain.
10. The ________ of Nations did nothing to stop German troops.
11. The German invasion of Austria went against the ________ of Versailles.
12. The Nazis terrorized Jews during the "________ of Broken Glass."

Name Date Period

Workbook Activity 110

Chapter 26, Lesson 3

The Beginning of World War II

Directions During the early years of World War II, the following statements might have been made by certain world leaders. After each statement, write *C* for Winston Churchill, *H* for Adolf Hitler, *R* for Franklin Roosevelt, or *S* for Joseph Stalin.

C Winston Churchill
H Adolf Hitler
R Franklin Roosevelt
S Joseph Stalin

1. "We will divide Poland with the Soviet Union." __________

2. "We must rescue the soldiers at Dunkirk." __________

3. "I shall insist that the RAF increase its defenses." __________

4. "We should consider lending arms to France and Great Britain." __________

5. "We must join the Allies, for Hitler wants to conquer Europe." __________

6. "Our island must defend itself at any cost." __________

7. "I believe this policy will keep us out of the war." __________

8. "I ask you to approve these funds to ready us for war." __________

9. "We will grant them rights to our naval and air bases." __________

10. "What? Is he forgetting our friendship treaty?" __________

11. "Too many bombers were destroyed. We'll have to change plans." __________

12. "We will stage a blitzkrieg." __________

13. "We must come to the aid of Poland." __________

14. "Like it or not, we'll have to begin a lottery for more soldiers." __________

15. "Using their bases, we can protect the Panama Canal." __________

War in Asia

Directions Use the words in the Word Bank to complete the paragraphs. Write each word on the correct line.

Word Bank

alliance	empire	naval fleet
ammunition	infamy	negotiations
battleships	Italy	oil
China	land	the Philippines
control	lend-lease	victory

America's Open Door Policy was threatened when Japan announced that it intended to rule all of Asia, including **1.** ____________________ . Japan continued its plan to create a(n) **2.** ____________________ . It went on to form a(n) **3.** ____________________ with Germany and Italy.

After Japan conquered Indochina, America became concerned that Japan was gaining too much **4.** ____________________ . In response, the United States stopped selling steel and **5.** ____________________ to Japan. In the meantime, America offered a(n) **6.** ____________________ program to China. Japan's Prime Minister Fumimaro Konoye and Secretary of State Cordell Hull failed at **7.** ____________________ .

On December 7, 1941, 353 Japanese airplanes set off to destroy the American **8.** ____________________ at Pearl Harbor. Within hours, the U.S. Pacific Fleet had lost many **9.** ____________________ , destroyers, and planes. More than 2,000 Americans had been killed. President Roosevelt referred to December 7 as a "date that will live on in **10.** ____________________ ." Japan's allies, Germany and **11.** ____________________ , soon declared war on the United States.

In **12.** ____________________ , American and Filipino troops fought the Japanese. Because the Filipinos and Americans lacked vehicles and **13.** ____________________, Japan gained another **14.** ____________________ . Japan had **15.** ____________________ of the Philippines.

The Home Front

Directions Match the words in Column 1 with the details in Column 2. Write the letter on the line.

Column 1

_____ **1.** volunteers

_____ **2.** industries

_____ **3.** General Motors

_____ **4.** African Americans

_____ **5.** bacon grease

_____ **6.** underestimate

_____ **7.** shortages

_____ **8.** women

_____ **9.** fear and prejudice

_____ **10.** victory gardens

_____ **11.** gunpowder bags

_____ **12.** detention camps

_____ **13.** Japanese American soldiers

_____ **14.** ration

_____ **15.** posters

Column 2

A caused the nation to set aside democratic principles

B to use less or limit the amount of something

C to guess the importance of something as being less than it is

D were made from worn nylon stockings

E served in every military role except combat

F needed raw materials to make war supplies

G produced one-third of the nation's vegetables

H were used to hold Japanese Americans against their will

I changed styles of people's clothes

J was able to make more war supplies than all of Germany and Japan

K fought bravely in Europe

L reminded Americans of their duty

M collected tires, cans, and papers

N was used for making ammunition

O faced job discrimination in the defense industry

Germany and Japan Surrrender

Directions The statements in the Answer Bank describe the final events of World War II. However, they are in the wrong order. Rewrite them on the lines below in the order in which they occurred.

Answer Bank

- President Roosevelt dies.
- Allied leaders meet in Yalta.
- President Roosevelt begins his fourth term.
- The United States drops two atomic bombs.
- Japan surrenders.
- The Battle of the Bulge begins.
- President Truman gives a last warning to Japan.
- Germany surrenders.
- The Allies capture Sicily and Rome.
- Allied troops land at Normandy on D-Day.

1. ______________________________

2. ______________________________

3. ______________________________

4. ______________________________

5. ______________________________

6. ______________________________

7. ______________________________

8. ______________________________

9. ______________________________

10. ______________________________

Name Date Period

A Growing Economy

Directions Write the correct word from the Word Bank to completeeach sentence.

Word Bank

baby boom	irrigation
Employment	middle class
farmers	suburbs
gas-powered tractors	unemployment
GI Bill	white-collar

1. When 12 million soldiers returned home, people feared ______________________.

2. Congress passed the Full ______________________ Act to help the economy.

3. The ______________________ helped former soldiers go to college.

4. Millions of new homes were built in the ______________________.

5. Because of the ______________________, more schools had to be built.

6. By the 1960s, America had a large ______________________ of people who owned homes and cars.

7. Many people worked at ______________________ jobs in offices.

8. American ______________________ became the most productive in the world.

9. Thanks to ______________________, farmers produced more crops faster.

10. Farmers could get water to their fields with modern ______________________ systems.

Name Date Period

War and Peace

Directions Write the answers to these questions. Use complete sentences.

1. How many American men and women did the United States lose in World War II?

2. What five nations were made permanent members of the United Nations Security Council in 1945?

3. What were four features of President Truman's "Fair Deal"?

4. What did the Taft-Hartley Act allow employers to do?

5. In the 1948 election, which groups of voters supported Truman?

Name Date Period

Cold War Crossword

Directions Read each clue. Then choose the correct word from the Word Bank to complete the puzzle.

Word Bank

- airlift
- Berlin
- Churchill
- cold war
- containment
- domination
- Eisenhower
- four
- Greece
- Iron
- Marshall
- NATO
- Soviet
- Truman
- Yalta

Across

3. _______ developed a policy to contain Communism.

7. _______ was the first head of the NATO force.

9. After World War II, the United States began a struggle with the _______ Union.

10. In 1949, several countries formed an alliance called _______.

11. President Truman ordered a(n) _______ of supplies to Berlin.

13. Winston Churchill said that an "_______ Curtain has descended" across Europe.

14. The conflict between Western nations and the Soviet Union was called the _______.

15. The Soviet Union did not keep the promises of the _______ Agreement.

Down

1. The United States feared that the Soviet Union wanted world _______.

2. _______ had a civil war after World War II.

4. The Soviet Union closed off the German city of _______.

5. Secretary of State _______ wanted America to help with the rebuilding of Europe.

6. _______ challenged the United States to stop the spread of Communism.

8. The U.S. policy of _______ helped Turkey and Greece defeat Communist forces.

12. Germany was divided into _______ sections after World War II.

Name Date Period

The Korean War

Directions Use the words in the Word Bank to complete the paragraphs. Write each word on the corrrect line.

Word Bank

boycotting	General MacArthur	Seoul
China	Manchuria	Soviet Union
Communists	President Truman	United Nations
Congress	Pusan	United Nations Security Council
Democratic People's Republic	Republic of Korea	United States

After World War II, Korea was divided into two parts. The northern section was held by the **1.** ______________________, while the south was controlled by the **2.** ______________________. America withdrew its troops when the **3.** ______________________ was set up. North Korea became the Communist-controlled **4.** ______________________.

After North Korea invaded South Korea, the **5.** ______________________ announced that the move was wrong. The Security Council asked the **6.** ______________________ to help South Korea. Because they had been **7.** ______________________ that organization, the Soviet Union was unable to veto the plan of action. **8.** ______________________ sent American troops to help South Korea.

North Korea captured the South Korean capital of **9.** ______________________.
10. ______________________ set up a defensive line of American troops at the port of **11.** ______________________. He and his troops were able to push the North Korean army toward the Chinese province of **12.** ______________________.

General MacArthur asked President Truman for permission to bomb **13.** ______________________. When Truman refused, MacArthur went to **14.** ______________________. As a result, Truman fired him.

Peace talks began in July of 1951. Both North and South Korea withdrew from their battle line. The North Koreans and Chinese who opposed the **15.** ______________________ were able to remain in South Korea.

Challenges in the 1950s

Directions Match the words in Column 1 with the details in Column 2. Write the letter on the line.

	Column 1		Column 2
______	**1.** Korean War veterans	**A**	used the fear of Communism for political gain
______	**2.** Rosa Parks	**B**	opened new career choices
______	**3.** Earl Warren	**C**	threatened American peace and security
______	**4.** Martin Luther King Jr.	**D**	wanted change in the 1952 election
______	**5.** National Guard	**E**	were buying new homes
______	**6.** advances in technology	**F**	became the first African American on the Supreme Court
______	**7.** bomb shelters	**G**	wrote that separate can never be equal
______	**8.** Dwight D. Eisenhower	**H**	was called to protect a Little Rock school
______	**9.** *Sputnik* and *Sputnik 2*	**I**	offered a higher standard of living
______	**10.** Joseph McCarthy	**J**	entertained young children on television
______	**11.** Republicans	**K**	led a bus boycott and spoke against discrimination
______	**12.** Howdy Doody	**L**	were launched before the first U.S. satellite
______	**13.** Thurgood Marshall	**M**	was elected president in 1952 by a landslide
______	**14.** nuclear war	**N**	challenged segregation by staying in her bus seat
______	**15.** women's movement	**O**	were built in many backyards

The 1960s Begin

Directions Write the answers to these questions. Use complete sentences.

1. What did John Glenn do in 1962?

____

____

____

2. Why didn't President Eisenhower run for re-election in 1960?

____

____

____

3. Who was the Republican candidate in the 1960 election? What political experience did this man have?

____

____

____

4. What role did television play in the 1960 presidential election?

____

____

____

5. What two things about President Kennedy made him a unique president?

____

____

____

Supporting Freedom Abroad

Directions The statements below might have been made by world leaders during the early 1960s. Decide which leader might have made each statement. After the statement, write *JK* for John F. Kennedy, *NK* for Nikita Khrushchev, or *FC* for Fidel Castro.

JK John F. Kennedy
NK Nikita Khrrushchev
FC Fidel Castro

1. "It is time to force them out of West Berlin." __________
2. "I just received a letter from the premier about the Cuban missiles." __________
3. "The United States will not leave Berlin." __________
4. "Our new communist government needs your help." __________
5. "I think he is too young and inexperienced." __________
6. "I will authorize the training, but no other participation." __________
7. "We have killed or captured most of the invaders." __________
8. "I don't care if it belongs to Americans. Seize it!" __________
9. "We will build a dividing wall." __________
10. "I led the revolt against our dictator." __________
11. "You must give me your word that you will not invade Cuba." __________
12. "I take full responsibility for the failed Bay of Pigs invasion." __________
13. "The navy must stop those ships." __________
14. "I order our ships to return at once." __________
15. "We have discovered that Cuba has hidden missiles." __________

Civil Rights Crossword

Directions Read each clue. Then choose the correct word from the Word Bank to complete the puzzle.

Word Bank

Equality
King
Meredith
riots
schools
segregation
tactic
violent
voting
Washington

Across

4. The March on _______ was in support of the civil rights bill.

6. _______ over segregation broke out at the University of Mississippi.

8. Dr. Martin Luther _______ Jr. spoke about his dream for America.

9. The Civil Rights Act protected the _______ rights of African Americans.

10. The Civil Rights Act allowed the government to speed desegregation in _______.

Down

1. James Farmer, who led the freedom riders, was from the Congress of Racial _______.

2. The freedom riders wanted to draw attention to _______ in southern states.

3. Television cameras captured the _______ response to peaceful protests.

5. James _______ was protected by U.S. troops at the University of Mississippi.

7. One _______ that civil rights protesters used was the sit-in.

The Johnson Administration

Directions Write the correct word from the Word Bank to complete each sentence.

Word Bank	
federal government	Tonkin Gulf
Great Society	previous presidents
Medicare	Urban
Paris, France	Vietcong
Poverty	South Vietnam

1. President Johnson challenged America to wage a "War on ____________________."

2. During the 1964 presidential campaign, Johnson challenged the people to make America a "____________________."

3. Johnson's opponent, Senator Barry Goldwater, felt that the ____________________ should not interfere in states' policies.

4. Johnson's ____________________ plan provided health insurance for the elderly.

5. Robert Weaver was appointed head of the new Department of Housing and ____________________ Development.

6. Johnson decided to expand America's role in an Asian country called ____________________.

7. ____________________ had sent only weapons, economic aid, and advisors to Vietnam.

8. The approval of Congress to "take all necessary measures" to protect American forces was called the ____________________ Resolution.

9. As ____________________ groups were destroyed, they were replenished by North Vietnamese.

10. In 1969, a meeting of leaders from North and South Vietnam, the United States, and the Vietcong was held in ____________________.

Name Date Period

New Movements in America

Directions Match the words in Column 1 with the details in Column 2. Write the letter on the line.

Column 1

_____ **1.** Malcolm X

_____ **2.** Equal Rights Amendment

_____ **3.** migrant

_____ **4.** Stokely Carmichael

_____ **5.** Nobel Peace Prize

_____ **6.** baby boomers

_____ **7.** American Indian Movement

_____ **8.** Vietnam War involvement

_____ **9.** hippies

_____ **10.** college students

_____ **11.** Woodstock

_____ **12.** Black Power

_____ **13.** counterculture

_____ **14.** feminists

_____ **15.** Cesar Chavez

Column 2

A youth culture that promoted freedom from social rules

B peaceful New York rock concert

C wore long hair, listened to rock music, and "did their own thing"

D wanted more control over their studies

E believed African Americans should control their communities

F said African Americans needed Black Power

G fought for women's rights

H movement that promoted African American heritage

I was passed by many states

J was challenged by many young people

K organized Mexican American migrants

L demanded better opportunities for American Indians

M were born right after World War II

N travels from place to place for work

O was awarded to Martin Luther King Jr.

The Politics of Protest

Directions Each statement in the Answer Bank might have been said about American leaders during the 1960s. Write each statement under the correct heading below.

Answer Bank

- He was elected with less than half the popular vote.
- He decided not to seek re-election.
- The party that nominated him was divided.
- He promised an end to the Vietnam War.
- He died while campaigning for president.
- He wanted to "Bring Us Together."
- Many felt he would follow Johnson's policies.
- He was shot in Memphis, Tennessee.
- He tried to please the hawks and the doves.
- His death led to angry riots.

Robert Kennedy

1. ______________________________

Martin Luther King Jr.

2. ______________________________

3. ______________________________

Lyndon Johnson

4. ______________________________

5. ______________________________

Hubert Humphrey

6. ______________________________

7. ______________________________

Richard Nixon

8. ______________________________

9. ______________________________

10. ______________________________

The Vietnam War Moves into Cambodia

Directions Put the events in order. Write *1* on the line beside the event that happened first. Write *2* beside the event that happened second. Continue to 10.

______ **A** American troops went into Cambodia to destroy enemy supplies.

______ **B** The news of U.S. military involvement in Cambodia caused protests.

______ **C** The National Guard began shooting at the protesters.

______ **D** Student protesters ended up burning a building at Kent State University.

______ **E** The U.S. Senate ended financial and military support for Cambodia.

______ **F** The Vietcong set up bases in Cambodia.

______ **G** The governor of Ohio sent in the National Guard.

______ **H** North Vietnam gained control of northeastern Cambodia.

______ **I** Students threw rocks at National Guard soldiers.

______ **J** Four students at Kent State University were killed.

Détente with China and the Soviet Union

Directions Match the words in Column 1 with the descriptions in Column 2. Write the letter on the line.

Column 1

_____ **1.** Henry Kissinger

_____ **2.** SALT

_____ **3.** Moscow

_____ **4.** Leonid Brezhnev

_____ **5.** détente

_____ **6.** Chou En-lai

_____ **7.** Richard Nixon

_____ **8.** strategic

_____ **9.** rival

_____ **10.** Taiwan government

Column 2

A first U.S. president to visit the Soviet Union in peacetime

B well-matched opponent

C President Nixon's top foreign policy adviser

D government of China in the 1950s and 1960s according to America

E city that Nixon visited in the Soviet Union

F president of the Soviet Union

G premier of China

H French word meaning "relaxation"

I treaty limiting U.S. and Soviet strategic weapons

J important or helpful in carrying out a plan

Name Date Period

Watergate Crossword

Directions Read each clue. Then choose the correct word from the Word Bank to complete the puzzle.

Word Bank

- aides
- conspiracy
- Cox
- evidence
- five
- Ford
- impeached
- judgments
- Liddy
- oath
- resigned
- Senate
- subpoena
- Watergate
- wiretaps

Across

2. Archibald _______ was the special prosecutor that Nixon fired.

4. Gordon _______ made a proposal to spy on the Democrats.

6. In June 1972, _______ burglars broke into a Democratic office.

7. Vice President Spiro Agnew _______ in October 1973.

8. Nixon did not want to be _______, so he resigned.

10. Two of Nixon's top _______ resigned, and another aide was fired.

12. Nixon said some of his _______ were wrong.

13. The court issued a(n) _______ for certain tapes.

Down

1. _______ is the name of a building in Washington, D.C.

2. The burglars acted together and were convicted of _______.

3. The burglars wanted to photograph documents and place _______.

5. Both _______ and House committees investigated.

6. Gerald _______ said that the U.S. Constitution works.

9. _______ found in records showed that Nixon was guilty.

11. James McCord said that he had lied under _______.

The Ford Administration

Directions Use the words in the Word Bank to complete the paragraphs. Write each word on the correct line.

Word Bank		
bicentennial	Israel	sailing ships
criticized	Mars	shocked
embargo	pardoned	United States
gas stations	prices	*Viking I*
heating oil	Queen Elizabeth	Watergate

Shortly after becoming president, Gerald Ford **1.** ______________________ Richard Nixon. Ford felt the nation needed to forget **2.** ______________________. He was **3.** ______________________ for this action.

During a conflict between Arab states and **4.** ______________________, some Arab states placed a(n) **5.** ______________________ on oil shipments to many countries, including the United States. Americans had to wait in long lines at **6.** ______________________. There was a shortage of home **7.** ______________________. Americans were **8.** ______________________ at how dependent they were on other countries. The Organization of Petroleum Exporting Countries began to regulate oil **9.** ______________________. This drove up the price of gasoline and heating oil in the **10.** ______________________.

On July 4, 1976, America celebrated the **11.** ______________________ of its Declaration of Independence. **12.** ______________________ presented America with a six-ton bell. More than 200 large **13.** ______________________ came from 30 nations. Two weeks after the celebration, the spaceship **14.** ______________________ successfully landed on **15.** ______________________.

Problems Around the World

Directions Use the names in the Word Bank to complete the chart. Write each name in the correct box.

Word Bank			
Anastasio Somoza	Egypt	Jimmy Carter	Nicaragua
Anwar Sadat	El Salvador	Lebanon	Panama
Oscar Romero	Israel	Menachem Begin	United States

Country	Leader	Description
1.	**2.**	had high inflation and an energy crisis
3.		signed two treaties with the United States in 1977
4.	**5.**	had a civil war; a leader was overthrown
6.	**7.**	had political violence in 1980; a religious leader was assassinated
8.	**9.**	attempted to make peace with Israel's government in 1977
10.	**11.**	had conflicts with Arab neighbors; signed a peace treaty with Egypt
12.		had many PLO members living there; was bombed by Israel

Name Date Period

Workbook Activity 130
Chapter 29, Lesson 6

International Problems Continue

Directions Write the answers to the questions. Use complete sentences.

1. Why were Iranians upset with the shah?

____

____

____

2. Explain how the government of Iran changed in 1979.

____

____

____

3. What did President Carter do that upset the Iranian people?
How did they show their anger?

____

____

____

4. What did the Soviet Union do in Afghanistan, and what happened there?
How did the United States show it was unhappy with Soviet actions?

____

____

____

5. Why didn't the U.S. Senate ratify the SALT II treaty?

____

____

____

Name Date Period

President Reagan's First Term

Directions Write the answers to these questions. Use complete sentences.

1. What happened to the 52 American hostages in Iran on the day President Reagan took office?

____

____

____

2. What happened to Ronald Reagan on his 70th day in office?

____

____

____

3. What act, suggested by President Reagan, provided tax and budget cuts?

____

____

____

4. How did Justice O'Connor believe the Supreme Court should interpret the Constitution?

____

____

____

5. How long had the space shuttle *Challenger* been in the air before it exploded?

____

____

____

Name Date Period

Workbook Activity 132
Chapter 30, Lesson 2

President Reagan's Second Term

Directions Read each clue. Then choose the correct word from the Word Bank to complete the puzzle.

Word Bank

- apartheid
- Congress
- contras
- *Discovery*
- explosives
- Gadhafi
- Gorbachev
- Iraq
- Lebanon
- Nicaragua
- Persian
- Sadat
- sanction
- South Africa
- terrorists

Across

1. Space shuttle that successfully carried five astronauts in 1988
3. Libyan leader who was blamed for terrorist attacks
7. Country with Palestinian bases where 200 U.S. soldiers were killed
9. People responsible for airport attacks in Rome and Vienna
12. Nicaraguan rebels who received U.S. support
13. Egyptian president who was assassinated in 1981
14. Soviet leader who wanted openness
15. Country with a white government that denied rights to the majority

Down

2. Country that fired a missile into the *USS Stark*
4. Policy of racial segregation in South Africa
5. U.S. governing body that was shocked by the contra scandal
6. Gulf where the U.S. Navy protected shipping lanes
8. Country in Central America that had a Communist government
10. Devices that caused a truck to explode at a marine base
11. Action taken to force a country to do something

Name ________________ Date ________ Period ________

Workbook Activity 133
Chapter 30, Lesson 3

Social Issues and the Bush Administration

Directions Match the words in Column 1 with the details in Column 2. Write the letter on the line.

	Column 1		Column 2
______	**1.** large deficit	**A**	1988 Republican presidential candidate
______	**2.** Douglas Wilder	**B**	result of a decline in men's wages
______	**3.** Colin Powell	**C**	country that finally let its citizens leave if they wished
______	**4.** Soviet Union	**D**	1988 Democratic presidential candidate
______	**5.** United States	**E**	problem caused by federal government spending
______	**6.** cold war	**F**	first African American mayor of New York City
______	**7.** women workers	**G**	conflict that seemed to be ending as Communism fell
______	**8.** two-income families	**H**	result of a shortage of low-cost housing
______	**9.** David Dinkins	**I**	country that had economic problems in the 1980s
______	**10.** East Germany	**J**	top military officer in the United States
______	**11.** Jesse Jackson	**K**	country that had banking problems, crime, and drug abuse
______	**12.** homelessness	**L**	first African American governor of Virginia
______	**13.** George Bush	**M**	German city divider that was removed
______	**14.** Michael Dukakis	**N**	new and important part of the American economy
______	**15.** Berlin Wall	**O**	first African American presidential candidate

The Fall of Communism

Directions Write the answers to these questions. Use complete sentences.

1. Which three former Soviet republics were the first to join the Commonwealth of Independent States?

____

____

____

2. Who were the three presidents of Russia from 1990 through 2000?

____

____

____

3. What were glasnost and perestroika?

____

____

____

4. Which republics are called the Baltic States?

____

____

____

5. Which three countries had been under Soviet control but declared their independence by the early 1990s?

____

____

____

Gulf War Crossword

Directions Read each clue. Then choose the correct word from the Word Bank to complete the puzzle.

Word Bank

allies
Arab
Baker
bombs
casualty
common
deadline
diplomats
Hussein
Kuwait
oil
peace
resource
Schwarzkopf
Storm

Across

1. "Operation Desert Shield" became "Operation Desert ________."

4. The Iraqi leader was Saddam ________.

8. The commander of the allied forces was Norman ________.

10. A ________ is someone who is killed, wounded, or lost in combat.

12. Allied planes rained ________ on Iraq and Iraqi forces in Kuwait.

14. The UN Security Council gave Iraq a ________ to leave Kuwait.

15. People skilled at negotiating between nations are ________.

Down

2. Many worried about one nation controlling an important natural ________.

3. Before the war, some nations agreed to raise the price of ________.

5. Iraq invaded ________ in August 1990.

6. By involving Israel, Hussein tried to force ________ nations to join him.

7. Iraq was a ________ enemy of Arab and Western nations.

9. President Bush wanted to bring lasting ________ to the Middle East.

11. The United States and its ________ attacked Iraq by air and on land.

13. Secretary of State James ________ met with Middle East leaders.

The Clinton Administration

Directions Match the words in Column 1 with the details in Column 2. Write the letter on the line.

Column 1

_______ **1.** Brady Bill

_______ **2.** George Bush

_______ **3.** Hillary Rodham Clinton

_______ **4.** Congress

_______ **5.** Omnibus Violent Crime Control and Prevention Act

_______ **6.** Bill Clinton

_______ **7.** unemployment rate

_______ **8.** tariffs

_______ **9.** Ross Perot

_______ **10.** Al Gore

_______ **11.** Arkansas

_______ **12.** 1993 deficit bill

_______ **13.** Democrats

_______ **14.** NAFTA

_______ **15.** Carol Mosely-Braun

Column 2

A led to more U.S. exports to Canada and Mexico

B was the first African American woman elected to the Senate

C set up a computer network to check gun buyers

D became the vice president in 1993

E kept control of Congress

F included tax increases and federal budget cuts

G rejected changes to the health care system

H was defeated by Democrat Bill Clinton

I banned certain weapons and allowed more local police

J lost its governor in the 1992 presidential election

K was at an eight-year high

L had many votes as an independent candidate

M were removed from U.S. goods coming into Mexico

N stressed the need for a better economy and won the election

O proposed that employers pay most of employee insurance costs

Name Date Period

President Clinton Faces Foreign Issues

Directions Each statement in the Answer Bank describes a foreign country during the 1990s. Write the letter of each statement after the correct country below.

Answer Bank

A Its leader was removed from office and met with President Clinton.

B 20,000 of its citizens could come to America each year.

C Its prime minister and a PLO leader met at a U.S.-hosted summit.

D President Clinton and its leader agreed about strategic weapons.

E Heavy casualties from a civil war forced U.S. troops to leave it.

F U.S. sanctions on it helped to end apartheid.

G President Clinton sent warships and troops to restore its government.

H President Clinton announced full diplomatic relations with it.

I The United States promised to protect it in case of attack.

J Its leader signed a peace treaty, ending a 46-year war.

K It was part of the former Yugoslavia, and a three-way war began in it.

L Its people were starving, so UN troops brought them food.

M Its president agreed to take down its nuclear arsenal.

N America sent it food and medicine by parachute.

O Nelson Mandela became its first black president.

Somalia: _______ and _______

Israel: _______ and _______

Russia: _______

Ukraine: _______ and _______

South Africa: _______ and _______

Vietnam: _______

Bosnia-Herzegovina: _______ and _______

Haiti: _______ and _______

Cuba: _______

Name Date Period

National Issues During the Clinton Years

Directions Write the correct term from the Word Bank to complete each sentence.

Word Bank

Contract	insurance companies	re-elected
federal budget	Million Man March	Robert Dole
federal government	minimum wage bill	Timothy McVeigh
hate and racism	Oklahoma City	Whitewater Affair
impeached	poverty	World Trade Center

1. In 1994, a Republican plan called the "________________ with America" was introduced.

2. A bill that called for a balanced ________________ by 2002 was rejected by the Senate.

3. A new law required the ________________ to pay for the cost of demands made on states.

4. In the ________________, the Clintons faced accusations but denied illegal involvement.

5. In 1993, a bomb exploded in the garage of the ________________ in New York City.

6. In 1995, 169 people died when a bomb exploded near a federal building in

________________.

7. ________________ was executed for this terrorist bombing.

8. Hundreds of thousands of African American men took part in the ________________.

9. A welfare law gave more responsibility for dealing with ________________ to the states.

10. A new law said ________________ could not drop a customer due to a medical condition.

11. President Clinton believed that a(n) ________________ would result in stronger families.

12. In the 1990s, arsonists burned church buildings because of ________________.

13. In the 1996 election, ________________ and Ross Perot were presidential candidates.

14. Bill Clinton, the incumbent, was ________________ by a wide margin.

15. In 1998, the House ________________ Clinton, but the Senate acquitted him.

New Millennium Crossword

Directions Read each clue. Then choose the correct word from the Word Bank to complete the puzzle.

Word Bank

computers
Electoral
Florida
Green
Gore
Lieberman
millennium
oil
OPEC
popular
recount
Reform
Supreme
surplus
Texas

Across

2. Pat Buchanan was the _______ Party candidate.

4. The _______ Court made a decision in the 2000 election.

5. Many Americans blamed _______ for not increasing oil production.

9. A(n) _______ is a period of 1,000 years.

10. Al Gore won the _______ vote in the 2000 election.

12. George W. Bush was governor of _______.

13. People worried about the rising price of _______ and gas.

15. The _______ College meets to vote for the president.

Down

1. Ralph Nader was the _______ Party candidate.

3. _______ was the deciding state in the 2000 election.

6. People feared the Y2K Bug in _______.

7. Because of a close vote in Florida, a(n) _______ was required.

8. The budget _______ was a campaign issue.

11. Al Gore's running mate was Joseph _______.

14. The Democratic presidential candidate was Al _______.

Name ______ Date ______ Period ______

Workbook Activity 140
Chapter 32, Lesson 1

Terrorism in the United States

Directions Match the words in Column 1 with the descriptions in Column 2. Write the letter on the line.

	Column 1		Column 2
______	**1.** 9/11	**A**	symbol of America's economic power
______	**2.** patriotism	**B**	U.S. president in 2001
______	**3.** Patriot Act	**C**	symbol of America's military power
______	**4.** firefighters and police officers	**D**	terrorist group that attacked the United States in 2001
______	**5.** Rudy Giuliani	**E**	symbols of American democracy
______	**6.** hijacker	**F**	pride in one's country
______	**7.** World Trade Center	**G**	mayor of New York City in 2001
______	**8.** war on terrorism	**H**	planned violence to frighten people into meeting certain demands
______	**9.** Pentagon	**I**	antiterrorism law
______	**10.** White House and U.S. Capitol building	**J**	person who steals an occupied vehicle by force
______	**11.** terrorism	**K**	name given for the events that happened on September 11, 2001
______	**12.** Homeland Security	**L**	heroes who fought hijackers and died in a plane crash in Pennsylvania
______	**13.** George W. Bush	**M**	U.S. department that is responsible for protecting Americans
______	**14.** Al Qaeda	**N**	heroes who died trying to save people in the World Trade Center
______	**15.** passengers and crew	**O**	focus of President Bush's administration after 9/11

The War on Terror Begins

Directions Write the answers to these questions. Use complete sentences.

1. Describe Afghanistan under Taliban rule.

2. What demands did the United States and the United Nations make on Afghanistan and the Taliban?

3. Who helped U.S. and British troops fight the war in Afghanistan?

4. How did Afghanistan change after the war?

5. Why did the United States and Great Britain invade Iraq?

Name Date Period

Workbook Activity 142
Chapter 32, Lesson 3

What Happened After the War in Iraq?

Directions Write the correct word from the Word Bank to complete each sentence.

Word Bank		
Afghanistan	Iran	soldiers
captured	military	terrorists
democratic	rebuilt	United Nations
elections	repairs	weapons
graves	Saddam Hussein	years

1. After the main fighting ended in Iraq, U.S. and British ______________________ remained.

2. The soldiers were looking for ______________________ of mass destruction.

3. The soldiers found the ______________________ of thousands of murdered people.

4. The soldiers were also trying to find ______________________.

5. On December 13, 2003, American soldiers ______________________ Saddam Hussein.

6. The United States and other nations wanted Iraq to be a(n) ______________________ nation.

7. Iraq was poor because it fought a long war with ______________________ in the 1980s.

8. The Iraqi economy had to be ______________________.

9. Iraq's oil wells needed many costly ______________________.

10. At first, the United States did not ask for support from the ______________________.

11. Then ______________________ started killing American soldiers.

12. The United States and Great Britain asked the United Nations for more ______________________ and financial help.

13. President Bush also asked Congress for $87 billion to pay for the reconstruction of Iraq and ______________________.

14. Some people believe that U.S. troops will have to stay in Iraq for many ______________________.

15. Plans were put in place for ______________________ to be held in 2005.

The Presidential Candidates of 2004

Directions The statements below might have been made by President George W. Bush or Senator John Kerry during or after the election campaign of 2004. Decide which person could have made each statement. After each statement, write *B* for George W. Bush or *K* for John Kerry.

B George W. Bush
K John Kerry

1. "Iraq will soon have democratic elections." __________
2. "I will fight the war in Iraq differently." __________
3. "I will bring U.S. troops home much sooner." __________
4. "I got 286 electoral votes." __________
5. "I got 252 electoral votes." __________
6. "The war in Iraq is going in the right direction." __________
7. "I won 48 percent of the popular vote." __________
8. "We should have waited for UN sanctions to work in Iraq." __________
9. "I won the presidential election." __________
10. "I won the state of California." __________
11. "My running mate is Dick Cheney." __________
12. "My running mate is John Edwards." __________
13. "I won the electoral votes of 31 states." __________
14. "I won the state of Florida." __________
15. "I can do a better job than the current president." __________

Name Date Period

The United States Today

Directions Circle the letter of the answer that correctly completes each sentence.

1. In 2003, the space shuttle *Columbia* _______.

A exploded shortly after takeoff
B was the third brightest object in the night sky
C was on its first mission
D exploded right before it was scheduled to land

2. Astronauts and cosmonauts _______ the International Space Station.

A conduct experiments and take care of
B will soon be able to fly to Venus on
C died in an explosion on
D are unable to live on

3. One concern people have about technology is the way it leads to _______.

A a new standard of living
B advanced medical treatments
C a loss of privacy
D global warming

4. Satellite pictures of Earth today show _______.

A that the population is aging
B polluted water and air
C an increase in pesticide use
D melting ice at the poles

5. Trees are important because they _______.

A prevent floods and drought
B remove oxygen from the air
C turn oxygen into carbon monoxide
D turn carbon monoxide into oxygen

6. If the polar ice caps melt, _______.

A northern animals might drown
B coastal cities might be flooded
C global warming will be reversed
D billions of people might die

7. _______ the leading cause of air pollution.

A Scientists are still trying to identify
B Global warming is
C The burning of coal, oil, and natural gas is
D Farming and pesticide use are

8. _______ are in the "Rust Belt."

A Charlotte and Miami **B** Chicago and Miami **C** Detroit and Atlanta **D** Cleveland and Detroit

9. Globalization describes the _______.

A connection of world economies
B connection between world leaders
C worldwide influence of the United States
D economic influence of baby boomers

10. The aging of America means that _______.

A the land is getting harder to farm
B the U.S. political system needs updating
C the U.S. population is getting older
D we have the oldest democracy in the world